PRAISE FOR HAKI R. MADHUBUTI'S WORK

"Haki R. Madhubuti knows that nothing human is elegant. He is not interested in modes of writing that aspire to elegance. He is well acquainted with 'elegant' literature (what hasn't he read?) but, while certainly respecting the advant͏͏ ͏s and influence of good workmanship, he is not interested in suppl͏͏ ͏ of the English Departments at Harvard and Oxford, nor ͏ *Review*, although he could mightily serve as fact ͏ blacks hungry for what they themselves refe͏ themselves and the stuff of their existence in ͏ verse. The last thing these people crave is ele͏ elegant song, the ears of a fellow whose stom ͏͏ ͏ur you. The more interesting noise is too loud."

Gwendolyn Brooks
Winner of Pulitzer Prize and author of *Blacks*

"What is more needed than these poems celebrating our traditional selves, our long history of loving and being loved? Who better than Haki to continue to write them? A necessary book."

Lucille Clifton
Poet and author of *Generations: A Memoir*

"Haki Madhubuti has created warm elegant poems that give honor to his long life of community work and poetry. Some of the finest human poems in English are in this book: "In Our Tradition," "Jimmy Lee," "What Makes Him Happy," as well as the powerful poems for Gwendolyn Brooks and for "Grandfathers."

Robert Bly
Poet, author of *The Sibling Society* and *Iron John*

"Reading *YellowBlack* is so much like the experience of reading Haki Madhubuti's strongest poetry, especially in the first section—in his rendering of the world he grew up in and the people in it, particularly his mother, but also his father and sister and the 'Men of God.'... This memoir was such a moving and illuminating experience."

Ruby Dee
Distinguished actor, producer, director and author
of *My One Good Nerve* and *With Ossie and Ruby: In This Life Together*

"Haki Madhubuti, the 'Cultural' son of Gwendolyn Brooks, is by his very nature, a poet. This deeply moving and lyrical memoir of his growing years is an indelible piece of writing. It is deceptively simple: it is profoundly touching and revelatory. A lovely work."

Studs Terkel
Winner of the Pulitzer Prize and author
of *Race* and *Will the Circle be Unbroken?*

"Again and again, Haki Madhubuti gives us necessary words that shine bright light in challenging times."

Elizabeth Alexander

Poet, essayist, playwright, and author *American Sublime*

"Haki was never just a writer, the fire and focus were a Lee legacy, but from that launching pad Haki went on to pick up very specific political determination. His undefined "Scream" was quickly self-defined as a *Black Nationalist* wail. And like quite a few of the artists of our generation, touched by the flame thrower of the *Black Arts Movement.* Haki boldly numbered himself among activist artists. Not just a speaker, but a Doer!

But during the height of the *Black Arts-Black Power* years, Haki wrote poems that served as *guidon* to the struggle, but even more important, he was an activist in that struggle. By the time *Direction Score,* he had even gotten to the point of making keen analysis of that struggle and it should be clear that that is where the fire and clarity of his poetic works came from, the struggle itself. Haki and I were both members of the *Congress of African People*, the *African Liberation Support Committee* and we have argued, marched and fought with both friends and enemies and we have remained, with legendary bumps and shudders, comrades in struggle. Despite the fact that we have not agreed on an encyclopedia of things in the world."

Amiri Baraka

Author of *RAZOR*

"So there it is: promise of a creative period, a high point if you will, where the old Don L. Lee style merges with a mature control of what some might call the page poem. Now it is true that even when you hear the music, you may not move the same way you did or could thirty years ago. And it is rare, I imagine, for poets to peak in their sixties. But Haki Madhubuti, running hard past sixty-two, seems to be in position to get the job done. I wouldn't bet against him. He may jump around & startle the world—yet again."

Keith Gilyard

Author of *Voices of the Self*

"Haki Madhubuti is a legendary poet, towering educator and premiere institution builder for freedom for over fifty years in the American Empire. His sheer genius and bold will to fight against white supremacy sustain us in these difficult times. And, his profound love of black people as well as all oppressed people is real and rare as that of Malcolm X, this book is another grand gift to the world. He is the last of the few great ones."

Cornel West

Editor of *The Radical King: Martin Luther King, Jr.*

"For over half a century Haki Madhubuti has been on a mission of redemption and repair, an immense, continuing voyage into the country's murky heart. He's deployed his vast imagination again and again to illuminate the white lies embedded in the American dream, and he's created a dazzling body of work that encounters an animated, boisterous humanity longing to live fully and free. Dr. Madhubuti is a singular truth seeker, he's also our collective treasure."

William Ayers
Author of *Public Enemy: Confessions of an American Dissident*

"Haki's poetry stretched my conceptualization of and address to oppression and liberation, deprivation and desire, debilitating gender privilege and desperately abject ceremonies of survival. His work remains dedicated to social critique, honest and lyrical analysis of inequality, calls for commitment, tenderness, resolution, community, and love. Such nostrums echo Haki's voice and compassion to poetry fundamentally different in kind from classic English, American, and French repertoires. English, French, and American canons are often verse endorsed by literary critics and scholarly promulgators of so-called *universal* standards of poetic form and excellence. These self-fashioning "gate keepers" have sought to ignore or minimize Haki's indisputably formative role in creating space, techniques, audiences, and publishing venues for new forms of Black poetic articulation."

Houston A. Baker, Jr.
Author of *Betrayal: How Black Intellectuals Have Abandoned the Ideals of the Civil Rights Era*

"What is Haki Madhubuti's legacy? Poetry, surely. But more than that, his work is evidence of the labor and commitment that is demanded of activists and literary giants. This collection offers us the arc of his development as a voice—reactionary poet to reflective wordsmith. Merciless at times, Madhubuti is always in the process of exposing, celebrating, educating, indicting, satirizing and, most often, loving. That he loved black people is obvious. He does so through his selfless offering of healing words of wisdom and dynamic action plans rooted in history. But his love extends beyond American ghettos and gentrified urban enclaves, beyond the lost and wandering homeless, beyond hip-hop divas and fearless thugs serving time or holding down street corners spinning rhymes. His love is universal, reaching into the Diaspora like a cyclone to gather us up and return us to our true selves."

Lita Hooper
Author of *Art of Work: The Art and Life of Haki R. Madhubuti*

"The poetry of Haki Madhubuti represents an epoch that radically changed the nature, art, and creative purpose for composing poetry. Constructed during the Black Arts Movement, his poetry is a point of contrast for protest poetry from the Harlem Renaissance to the 1950s and it is an originator of contemporary spoken word and hip-hop lyricism."

Regina Jennings
Author of *Malcolm X and the Poetics of Haki Madhubuti*

ALSO BY HAKI R. MADHUBUTI

Poetry

Honoring Genius, Gwendolyn Brooks: The Narrative of Craft, Art, Kindness and Justice
Liberation Narratives: New and Collected Poems 1966-2009
Run Toward Fear: New Poems and A Poet's Handbook
HeartLove: Wedding and Love Poems
GroundWork: New and Selected Poems of Don L. Lee/Haki R. Madhubuti from 1966-1996
Killing Memory, Seeking Ancestors
Earthquakes and Sunrise Missions
Book of Life
Directionscore: New and Selected Poems
We Walk the Way of the New World
Don't Cry, Scream
Black Pride
Think Black

Non-Fiction

Taking Bullets: Terrorism and Black Life in Twenty-First Century America
YellowBlack: The First Twenty-One Years of a Poet's Life, A Memoir
ToughNotes: A Healing Call for Creating Exceptional Black Men
Claiming Earth: Race, Rage, Rape, Redemption: Blacks Seeking a Culture of
    Enlightened Empowerment
Dynamite Voices: Black Poets of the 1960s
Black Men: Obsolete, Single, Dangerous? The African American Family in Transition
From Plan to Planet: Life Studies: The Need for African Minds and Institutions
Enemies: The Clash of Races
A Capsule Course in Black Poetry Writing (co-author)
African Centered Education (co-author)
Kwanzaa: A Progressive and Uplifting African American Holiday

Edited Works

Eighty Gifts: For Gwendolyn Brooks (limited edition, 2021)
Black Panther: Paradigm Shift or Not? (co-editor)
Not Our President: New Directions from the Pushed Out, the Others, and the Clear
    Majority in Trump's Stolen America (co-editor)
By Any Means Necessary, Malcolm X: Real, Not Reinvented (co-editor)
Releasing the Spirit: A Collection of Literary Works from Gallery 37 (co-editor)
Describe the Moment: A Collection of Literary Works from Gallery 37 (co-editor)
Million Man March/Day of Absence: A Commemorative Anthology (co-editor)
Confusion by Any Other Name: Essays Exploring the Negative Impact of The Black.
    Man's Guide to Understanding the Black Woman (editor)
Why L.A. Happened: Implications of the '92 Los Angeles Rebellion (editor)
Say That the River Turns: The Impact of Gwendolyn Brooks (editor)
To Gwen, With Love (co-editor)

Recordings: Poetry and Music

Liberation Narratives (with Nicole Mitchell and Black Earth Ensemble)
Rise Vision Comin' (with Nation: African Liberation Arts Ensemble)
Medasi (with Nation: African Liberation Arts Ensemble)
Rappin' and Readin'

TAUGHT
BY
WOMEN

TAUGHT BY WOMEN

POEMS AS RESISTANCE LANGUAGE
NEW AND SELECTED

Haki R. Madhubuti

THIRD WORLD PRESS

CHICAGO

Third World Press
Publishers since 1967
Chicago

First Edition
Printed in the United States of America

ISBN: 978-0-88378-358-0 | Paperback
ISBN: 978-0-88378-419-8 | Hardback

23 22 21 20   8 7 6 5 4 3 2 1

Library of Congress Cataloging-in-Publication
Names: Madhubuti, Haki R. 1942-
Title: Taught By Women
Description: First edition. I Chicago: Third World Press Foundation Books, 2020
Identifiers: ISBN   (hard cover; alkaline paper)
Subjects: LCSH: African American   Poetry I African American

Cover and interior layout by Borel Graphics
All photographs are part of the Haki R. Madhubuti Collection.

These poems have appeared in: *Chicago Review, African Voices, Chicago Sun Times, Poetry Magazine, Liberation Narratives, Honoring Genius, Don't Cry, Scream, Feminist Wire, The Chicago Reader, Run Toward Fear and Chicago Magazine, Claiming Earth, Black Women Writer's (1950-1980), Transforming a Rape Culture, Traps, Swaying in Wicked Grace: 25 Years of Furious Flower, The Best 100 African American Poems, Grandfathers and Taking Bullets.*

brothers, brothers
everywhere and
not a one
for sale.

Johari Amini

The freest people
in this world are
artists,
poets, fiction writers, visual artists,
musicians, actors, playwrights, photographers, composers,
dancers, choreographers, directors, and those who
create a language of possibilities, hope and
yes.

HRM

Women were regarded as no better
than the cows they milked.

Bogaletch Gebre
Ethiopian Human Rights worker who fought for
the elimination of the mutilation of female genitals.

I gave the brothers
anything they
wanted
if they wanted something.

Johari Amini

The answer to everything good is to put more women in power.

HRM

Stopping the women, stops the future.

HRM

Libraries and books are anti-ignorance.

HRM

RECENT REMEMBERING

RUBY DEE

TONI MORRISON

OCTAVIA BUTLER

NTOZAKE SHANGE

PAULE MARSHALL

JESSYE NORMAN

WHO ALSO HONORED WOMEN

JOHN LEWIS

LERONE BENNETT, JR.

CHADWICK BOSEMAN

C.T. VIVIAN

VINCENT HARDING

JOHN THOMPSON

RECENT EARTH CHANGERS

SANDRA BLAND

BREONNA TAYLOR

BOGALETCH GEBRE

Photo courtesy of Eugene Redmond

FOR DR. CAROL D. LEE/
MAMA SAFISHA MADHUBUTI
Perpetually Teaching Haki

DEDICATION II

For My Mother:
Maxine Graves Lee (deceased)

For My Wife:
Safisha Madhubuti (Carol D. Lee)
Ernestine Mims Lee (first wife, deceased)

For My Mother-in-law:
Inez Singleton Hall (deceased)

For My Daughters and their Mothers:
Regina Volcié Alcantar and Mother Joan LaMonthe
Mariama Lyotta Richards and Mother Leslie Richards
Laini Nzinga Madhubuti Lee

For My Daughters-in-law and their Mothers:
Janet Hutchinson Lee and Mother Judith Hutchinson
Janeen Lee and Mother Sheila Savory

For My Granddaughters:
Jazmin Sade Culpepper
Lajenne Volcié Alcantar
Layla Anaya Madhubuti Lee
Xiomara Inez Madhubuti Lee
Aminata Sun McLaurin Richards

For My Sister:
Jacqueline Lee

For My Sisters-in-law:
Valerie Hall and Marilyn Hall (deceased)

And For My Cultural Daughter:
Nicole Mitchell Gantt

TAUGHT BY WOMEN

CONTENTS

YELLOWBLACK

HEARTLOVE

YES: BLACK WOMEN

COMPLICATED MELODIES

WONDERMENT: LEAVING LARGE VOICES

ADDENDUM

POETRY MATTERS
AND MORE

WHY WOMEN?

Taught By Women is my acknowledgment and thank you to over half of the world's population who remain, too often property, raped, honor killed, diminished, enslaved, lynched, dismissed, excluded, lied to, abused, sexualized, sex trafficked, devalued, demeaned, executed, imprisoned, forgotten, forced into unwanted marriages, miseducated, undereducated, beheaded and bodily disfigured. All motivating me to be pro-girl and woman, which requires serious listening and specialized learning, advanced thought, care, action and language that highlights Black music, poetry and visual art which I received from my mother—a woman who worked and died in the sex trade of the 1950's. Just as capitalism, white supremacy, Black ignorance, enslavement and anti-religious thought killed her; I, her only son, am able today and tomorrow to act and state with finality, stop. And again thank you to Black women and the world of women for saving my life.

FOR THE CONSIDERATION OF POETS

where is the poetry of resistance,
    the poetry of honorable defiance
unafraid of the lies from career politicians and businessmen,
not respectful of journalists who write
official speak void of educated thought
without double search or sub surface questions
that war talk demands?
where is the poetry of doubt and suspicion
not in the service of the state, bishops and priests,
not in the service of beautiful people and late-night promises,
not in the service of influence, incompetence and academic
    clown talk?

ART II: Reviewing A Life, A Calling

among these senior words
this questioning and quieting narrative,
art, and all its imperfections, contributed wonderfully
to the defining history of my life: like why am I accused of being too Black,
sixties Black, but never too white?
as a doer in this world,
as a committed poet, political and cultural activist,
educator, publisher, questioning intellectual, business tryer,
husband, father, cultural father, word-organizer,
editor, institution builder, protector of children and pro street-fighter;
I have swum in an ocean not of my making.
after over seventy-eight years of an imperfected backstroke
I realized, the many countless times
I have been close to drowning, only to re-emerge stronger
in part due to the thousands of special and not so special people,
children, young voices and the children of children,
and the women who birthed them who
I have encountered in this life, in this struggle, on many continents.
I am here because of poetry. Black poetry and poetry of all cultures
in its multitudes of forms, laced with an abundance of content,
critical meaning, and local selves.

word-play, rhymes and unrhymes, metered, unmetered and off-metered, lines
and stanzas defined and undefined, packed with knowledge, information, laughter,
occasional wisdom and a patch quilt of voices that directed my young life, poetry.
certainly, starting at fourteen and searching for all kinds of answers, surrounded
by adults who could not manage their own lives. poetry and music stopped me in
my negative and ill directed back rooms. poetry and music slowly demanded that
I change paths, contemplate the dangers before me with a limited understanding
of the political, economic and cultural forces & faces that I was born into. these
multiple forces & faces were created to trap young people like me positioning us
in a *can't do philosophy* that many carried into adulthood and far too many,
a spiritless eldership. some were able to arrive into an honored elderhood,
however for unnoticed millions who slowly yet deliberately moved into an angry
and often early death were neglected and forgotten.

for me, reading and rereading and eventually studying the works of Wright, Hughes, Toomer, M. Walker, Brooks, Tolson, McKay, S. Brown, Bontemps, Hayden, Du Bois, Evans, Baldwin, Robeson, A. Locke, F.M. Davis, Cullens, Frazier, Woodson, Garvey, B.T. Washington, Hurston, Diop. Clarke, Davis and Dee, Dunbar, Douglass, Malcolm, H.W. Fuller, Fanon, Cruse and countless others in and outside of my culture confirmed in me that any people who control and define their own cultural and political imperatives and as a result of such intellectual influences, should be about the healthy replication of themselves and the world they
walk in. implanting in me the recognition that
without art in abundance
without art that provides new names and forms,
during the absence of love and grits,
during the years of bottomless lies, legal betrayals and enormous deaths,
without the maintenance and nurturing of early spirits that the music of Armstrong, Ellington, Trane, Simone, Miles, Holiday, Ella, Gillespie, Gaye, Motown, Fela, Philadelphia Sound, Scott-Heron, AACM, The Dells, Wonder, Mayfield, from Doo-Wop, to Nikki Mitchell & Black Earth Ensemble.

Through music that everyday art mandates, my life would have continued to evolve around reactions to:
the alphabet of hourly timecards,
embracing of corporate white nationalism
        fast walking urban street double-eyed
        the ignorance of demeaning the others and their otherness
        thinking that "citizens united" is actually pro-citizens
        locating identity in wearing labeled clothes, multicolored
        fingernails and pants below the crack of one's ass.
        aware of jim crow and ignorant of jane crow.
        unaware that the creation, wealth and building of America
        exists upon indigenous people's stolen land and African people's stolen
        intelligence and labor.

without wonder words, involved music, inviting visuals and flying feet. without reading books, without serious study of life's hopes and tangibles children will drink sports, rapper's realities, mall hopping consumption, twenty-four-hour cable surfing, all representing debilitating and limited information or knowledge needed to grow a superior intellect, families and tomorrows to save our planet. slow consumption. investigate veganism: one good nutritious meal a day. juice more. walk 3 miles a day. drink water. understand the kindness and language of gwendolyn brooks. in her quietness and poetry existed her religion and her life's work is summed up in "we are each other's harvest: we are each other's business: we are each other's magnitude and bond." losing gwendolyn brooks was like the destruction of a major library.

yet, what continues to energize these overworked bones are children of all cultures who for the most part have not been captured by the many demons, daggers and multiple predators that populate this earth. the absolute necessity in me to listen to young people, their laughter, tears, loud silences and demanding questions that are critical to my wellness. realizing that Black is human and humanizing, always requiring homework and deep study to do justice to who we really are.

but, quiet-as-its-kept, preceding all else, coming back to the stimulating juice that has fueled this life has been liberating ideas in resistant language as poetry, prose and richard pryor and moms mabley humor. equal to poetry and laughter has been music and visual art all slapping saneness, Black perspective, womanist and feminist, alertness, climate enlightenment, and anti-patriarchy thought and afterthought. a hunger for the unknown and a thousand questions into this yellowblack boy, teenager, young man, mature drinker of knowledge, and elder confirming and affirming that art works, humor works, Black culture works.

Black art works suggesting that white people's confirmed hatred of Black people is in direct conflict and contradiction to their love of Black culture. to call oneself a poet or artist like that of the black preacher, primary family doctor, veterinarian, farmer, or teacher of any branch of knowledge and to function at the highest order honoring one's choices and decisions is truly a *calling*.

we are, indeed defined by our yesterdays,
our here and now and tomorrows which finally acknowledges
and accepts the little appreciated fact
that for us, the poets, musicians, fiction writers, visual artists, playwrights, scholars,
wood and stone carvers, photographers, quilt makers, idea people, artists of all
disciplines; the real lovers of civilization and art are the freest people in the world.
and the exceptional children that are formed by art and culture
are here to stay and change the conversation, impact the saving of the *beautiful,*
highlighting the necessity of the small and large stories of this endangered planet.
that the Green New Deal must be First Thought, daily work and committed mis-

sion.
especially and lovingly in this era of the first Black president, which I, as many of my generation
clearly thought impossible, it is time to acknowledge that artists and their art and the demand on progressive thinking/acting that all good art requires played a pivotal and decisive role in making
possible the moving of the first African American/Black family into the white house. And they, represented the best commentary from the least of us we continue to influence and inspire our country's wholistic journey towards the inclusive ideas of liberation and yes for

the first woman to occupy that critical house.
for most artists there is no retirement,
there is no can't do or I forgot. but we remain with
an undying over-loving commitment to yes,
primarily
for all children of all cultures
while respectfully acknowledging
a realistic optimism, claiming
agency, beauty, definition, redefinition
and the absolute necessity of
Black. Blackness soulfully,
culturally, conscientiously, and in working
in all areas of creation while respecting that which is
good, just, correct, and right with an air of historical knowledge,
humility, dignity and strength.
forever struggling against the unbearable whiteness of
american culture, religion, systematic anti-Black violence & death.
making it extremely difficult, if not impossible
to love a country
that doesn't love you.
and as an artist and poet, never to disrespect
the freedoms that those who preceded us,
fought for us and partially achieved and passed on,
we seek an earth fed quest for liberation, smiles
and life itself
we have been put on notice and warned.

LIBERATION NARRATIVES

I. it may be
    a man's world   yet
    its women who write music
    that navigates the harmony that
    grows children, drives learning,
    prepare knives for the cutting of green beans & lies
    while dodging genocide & rape
    as men
    who run the world
    bathe in the power of extreme illusion
    overuse collateral-damage &
    deficit language to justify
    it's a man's world.

II. best advice to men
    marry women smarter than you!
    occasionally let them know it.

III. my mother was
    prettier than imagination soaked in
    honey flavored with
    hot water and lemon,
    her heart was there too.

    she was a short poem.

    dead at 34, buried without flowers
    notation or truthful stories.
    she challenged men walking on her life like
    she was a used treadmill years
    before they were invented.
    I have her eyes,
    I see damage everywhere,
    I have become a stop sign.

IV.　janet liked girls
and told them so,
robert liked boys
and kept it a secret.
both grew into teenagers
still liking girls,
still liking boys.
each kept their desires to themselves.
in the 21st century parts of the world
began to mature and finally
understood why
janet loved women
　　and
　　　　robert loved men.
　　　　they were born that way,
　　enough said.

V.　if poetry is to have meaning
it must mean something,
more than metaphor and simile,
more than tree-talk & looking for gigs,
more than competition in unrhymed free verse
serious to the bone of incomprehension
surely to land the poet
a guggenheim or macarthur genius grant.
artists should not expect from readers,
listeners and observers fairness, objectivity or
deep knowledge of wordplay or
interpreted ideas of paint or jumping notes.
often a smile will do, and yes
to buy and share books, visuals and music will help.
saying yes to children may get you into heaven,
saying no to war builds character and conscious,
giving ten percent of what you earn to the homeless
will aid in your sleeping a full night
hopefully to awake creating healthier
poems, prose, pictures &
critical perceptions of the

potential of the letter 'p' beyond politics,
potholes, profiteers, poverty, pimp juice, patriots,
protestants and playboys of the western world.

VI.   if you don't know
who you are,
anybody can
name you.

VII.   if the world loses elephants,
dolphins, polar bears, frogs, trees,
the ability of the majority to do good,
clean water, prayer & meditation in all languages,
love across borders, honest vegans & vegetarians,
a mother's love, a father's caring,
children dancing to knowledge & colors,
artists not lying for money, privilege or fame,
if the world loses books, newspapers,
clear thinkers, practical doers, poets,
promising futures for the great majority, rainforests,
a world vocabulary that accents yes & possibilities
rather than no and you can't do that,
if the world loses the great apes, schools,
giraffes, salmon, the coral reefs, insects,
worms, organic farmers, compost, green tea,
workers who use their hands
to build & repair stuff, north and south poles,
teachers, people of faith, engineers,
wheat-grass, carrot juice, oatmeal and seven grain bread.

if the world loses you and water,
yes, precious you and the daily taste of life
it finally means that
we've lost butterflies yesterday

and failed our children.

for Tarana Burke & #MeTooMovement

POETRY

Poetry will not stop or delay wars, will not erase rape
      from the landscape,
will not cease murder or eliminate poverty, hunger or
excruciating fear. Poems do not command armies, run
school systems or manage money. Poetry is not
intimately involved in the education of psychologists,
physicians or smiling politicians.

in this universe
the magic   the beauty   the willful art of explaining
the world & you;
the timeless   the unread   the unstoppable fixation
with language & ideas;
the visionary   the satisfiable equalizer screaming for
the vitality of dreams   interrupting false calm
demanding fairness and a new   new world are the
poets and their poems.

Poetry is the wellspring of tradition, the bleeding
connector to yesterdays and the free passport to
 futures.
Poems bind people to language, link generations to
each other and introduce cultures to cultures.
Poetry, if given the eye and ear, can bring memories,
issue in laughter, rain in beauty and cure ignorance.
Language in the context of the working poem can
raise the mindset of entire civilizations, speak to two
year olds and render some of us wise.

To be touched by living poetry can only make us
  better people.
The determined force of any age is the poem, old as
ideas and as lifegiving as active lovers. A part of any
answer is in the rhythm of the people; their heartbeat
comes urgently in two universal forms, music and
poetry.

for the reader for the quiet seeker
for the many willing to sacrifice one syllable
mumblings and easy conclusions
poetry
can be that gigantic river
that allows one to recognize
in the circle of fire
the center of life.

GWENDOLYN BROOKS AND HAKI R. MADHUBUTI
(Early 1970's)

ART IV: *remembering Gwendolyn Brooks*

art has its own language, name and questions,
    has clear talk, justice and motivation.
art does not create itself,
    does not escape the daily windstorms,
    fires, gun blasts, ignorant mumblings
    or cruel misrepresentations of the
    rulers and their gate-keepers.
artists and their art are liberated souls
forever sprinting and searching in the world.
they do not see borders, walls or can't do
and when confronted with such
they quietly and questionably,
loudly and deliberately   with
pens, paper, computers, film, cameras, paint
canvas, phones, creative ideas and feet
run toward fear
without hesitation or limiting doubts
with good and loving intentions, struggle
to move all of us into the yes community of
life-centered people
as directed by their art, conscience and culture
while intentionally
advancing quality definitions of a
kind-based civilization and world.

for David J. Steiner, artist/filmmaker, December 23, 2016

POET: Gwendolyn Brooks at 70

as in music,
as in griots singing,
as in language mastered, matured
beyond melodic roots.

you came from the land of ivory and vegetation,
of seasons with large women guarding secrets.
your father was a running mountain,
your mother a crop-gatherer and God-carrier,
your family, earth grown waterfalls,
all tested, clearheaded, focused.
ready to engage.

centuries displaced in this land of denial and disbelief,
this land of slavery and sugar
diets,
of bacon breakfasts, short suns and long moons,
you sought memory and hidden ideas,
while writing the portrait of a battered people.

artfully you avoided becoming a literary museum,
side-stepped retirement and canonization,
gently casting a rising shadow over a generation of
urgent-creators waiting to make fire,
make change.

with the wind in your hand,
as in trumpeter blowing,
as in poet singing,
as in sister of the people, of the language,
smile at your work.

your harvest is coming in, bountifully.

GWENDOLYN BROOKS

she doesn't wear
costume jewelry
& she knew that walt disney
was/is making a fortune off
false eyelashes and that time magazine is the
authority on the knee/grow.
her makeup is total-real.

a negro english instructor called her:
       "a fine negro poet."
a whi-te critic said:
       "she's a credit to the negro race."
somebody else called her:
       "a pure negro writer."
johnnie mae, who's a senior in high school, said:
       "she & langston are the only negro poets we've
       read in school and i understand her."
pee wee used to carry one of her poems around in his
  back pocket;
       the one about being cool, that was befo pee wee
       was cooled by a cop's warning shot.

into the sixties
a word was born..........BLACK
& with black came poets
& from the poet's ball points came:
black doubleblack purpleblack blueblack been black was
black daybeforeyesterday blackerthan ultrablack super
black blackblack yellowblack niggerblack blackwhi-te man
blackthanyoueverbes 1/4 black unblack coldblack clear
black my mama's blackerthanyourmama pimpleblack fall
black so black we can't even see you black on black in
black by black technically black mantanblack winter
black cookblack 360degreeblack coalblack midnight
black when it's convenient rustyblack moonblack
black starblack summerblack electronblack spaceman

black shoeshineblack jimshoeblack underwearblack ugly
black auntjemima black uncleben's rice black williebest
black blackisbeautifulblack i justdiscoveredblack negro
black unsubstanceblack.

and everywhere
the lady "negro poet"
appeared the poets were there,
they listened & questioned
& went home feeling uncomfortable/unsound & so
        untogether
they read/re-read/wrote & re-wrote
& came back the next time to tell the
lady "negro poet"
how beautiful she was/is & how she had helped them
& she came back with:
        how necessary they were and how they've helped her.
        the poets walked & as space filled the vacuum between
        them & the
lady "negro poet"
u could hear one of the blackpoets say:
        "bro, they been callin that sister by the wrong name."

                                                    1968

19

AN AFTERWORD: for Gwen Brooks
(the search for the new-song begins with the old)

knowing her is not knowing her.

is not
autograph lines or souvenir signatures & shared smiles.
is not
pulitzers, poet laureates or honorary degrees
you see   we ordinary people
just know
ordinary people

to read gwen is to be,
to experience her in the *real*
is the same, she is her words,   *more*
like a fixed part of the world   is there
quietly penetrating all cultures
reminds us of a willie kgositsile love poem   or
isaac hayes singing *one woman.*

still she suggests more:
have u ever seen her home?
it's an idea of her: a brown wooden frame
trimmed in dark gray with a new screen door.
inside: looks like the lady owes everybody on the southside
                    nothing but books mama's books.
her home like her person is under-fed and small.

gwen:
pours smiles of african-rain
a pleasure well received among uncollected garbage cans
and heatless basement apartments.
her voice the needle for new songs
plays unsolicited messages: poets, we've all seen

poets, minor poets ruined by
minor fame.

1971

A MOTHER'S POEM

(for G.B.)

not often do we talk.
      destruction was to be mine at 28
      a bullet in the head   or
      wrong-handed lies that would lock
      me in pale cells that are designed to
      cut breathing and will.
you gave me maturity at daybreak
slashed my heart
and slowed the sprint toward extinction,
delayed my taking on the world alone.
you made living a laborious & loving commitment.

you shared new blood,
challenged mistaken vision,
suggested frequent smiles,
while enlarging life to more than
daily confrontations and lost battles
fought by unprepared poets.

not often did we talk.
your large acts of kindness shaped memory,
your caring penetrated bone & blood
and permanently sculptured a descendant.
I speak of you in smiles
and seldom miss a moment
to thank you for
saving a son.

1984

MOTHERS

"mothers are not to be confused with females who only birth babies"

mountains have less height
and
elephants less weight than
mothers who plan bright futures for their children
against the sewers of western life.

mothers making magical music miles from monster madness
are not news,
are not subject for doctorates.

how shall we celebrate mothers?
how shall we call them in the winter of their lives?
what melody will cure slow bones?
who will bring them worriless late-years?
who will thank them for hidden pains?

mothers are not broken-homes,
they are irreplaceable fire,
a kiss or smile at a critical juncture,
a hug or reprimand when doubts swim in,
a calm glance when the world seems impossible,
the back that America could not break.

mothers making magical music miles from monster madness
are not news,
are not subject for doctorates.

mothers instill questions and common sense,
urge mighty thoughts and lively expectations,
are impetus for discipline and intelligent work while
making childhood exciting, unforgettable and challenging,
mothers are preventative medicine
they are
women who hold their children all night to break fevers,

women who cleaned other folks' homes in order to give their
          children one,
women who listen when others laugh,
women who believe in their children's dreams,
women who lick the bruises of their children and
give up their food as they suffer hanger pains silently.

if mothers depart their precious spaces too early
values, traditions and bonding interiors are wounded,
morals confused, ethics unknown, needed examples absent
          and
crippling histories of other people's victories are passed on as
          knowledge.

mothers are not broken homes,
they are gifts
sharing full hearts, friendships and mysteries,
as the legs of fathers are amputated
mothers double their giving
having seen the deadly future of white flowers.

mothers making magical music miles from monster madness
are not news,
are not subject for doctorates

who will bring them juice in the sunset of their time?
who will celebrate the wisdom of their lives.
the centrality of their songs,
the quietness of their love,
the greatness of their dance?
it must be us,
able daughters, good
sons their cultural gift,
the fruits and vegetables of their medicine.

we must come like earth rich waterfalls.

*for Mittie Travis (1897-1989), Maxine Graves Lee (1924-1959),
Inez Hall (1920-2014) and Gwendolyn Brooks (1917-2000)*

THIS POET: Gwendolyn Brooks at Eighty

this poet, this genuine visionary,
this carrier of the human spirit,
this chronicler of the Blackside of life,
this kind and gentle person is the reason
we lend our voices to this day.

that other poets have championed good writing
and literature, have exposed evil
in the world, have contributed mightily of personal resources
to the young, to the would-be-writers,
to students and to the institutions of common good
is without a doubt. however,
the only poet who has made it a mission
to incorporate all of this and more into a wonderful and
dedicated lifestyle is gwendolyn brooks
without press releases, p.r. people or interpreters
from the academy the great work of this quiet poet
has touched a city, this state, our nation and the world.
her poetry, her children's books,
her essays and her autobiographies have given us an insight
into the complexities of the Black human condition
that few writers can match, yet we all try
she is our standard.
seventy years of writing do make a difference.

we gratefully and gracefully walk in her shadow,
not because she needs or requests that we do so;
it is that her work,
her outstanding contribution to black literary music
in this world that demands the best from the least of us.
at eighty she needs no introductions or encouraging words.
at eighty the notes she writes to herself
are more comprehensive and in larger letters.

at eighty her walk is slower and her eyesight less certain.
at eighty she loves silence, is never voiceless or alone,

at eighty, Blackness remains her star and
she alerts her readers always to the huge possibility
of knowing oneself, others,
and the mystery and joy of a full life.

she has approached 320 seasons
on her own terms.
she has taken the alphabet and structured a language.
she has walked thousands of miles carrying her own baggage.

she has done the work she aimed to do,
children call her "Mama Gwen" and memorize her lines.

that which is "incomplete" is at her home
on the dining room table, in neat piles
enclosed in all size packages,
opened and unopened,
here and only here is where she will always be behind

she is the last of the great
handwritten letter answerers and
she will not be able to keep up with this volume of
love.

June 7, 1997

GWENDOLYN BROOKS: America in the Wintertime

in this moment of orangutans, wolves and scavengers,
of high heat redesigning the north & south poles
and the wanderings of new tribes in limousines,
with the confirmations of liars, thieves, and get over artists,
in the wilderness of pennsylvania avenue,
standing rock, misspelled executive orders
on yellow paper with crooked signatures.

where are the kind language makers among us?

at a time of extreme climate damage,
deciphering fake news, alternative truths and me-ism
you saw the 21st century and left us
not on your own accord or permission.
you have fought and fought most of the 20th century
creating an army of poets who learned
and loved language and stories
of complicated rivers, seas and oceans.

where is the kind green nourishment of kale and wheatgrass?

you thought, wrote and lived poetry,
knew that terror is also language based
on denial, first-ism and rich cowards.
you were honey and yes to us,
never ran from Black as in bones, Africa,
blood and questioning yesterdays and tomorrows.
we never saw you dance but you had rhythm,
you were a warrior before the war,
creating earth language, uncommon signs and melodies
and did not sing the songs of career slaves.

keenly aware of tubman, douglass, wells-barnett, du bois
and the oversized consciousness and commitment of never quit people
religiously taking note of the blood-lust enemies of kindness
we hear your last words:

america
if you see me as your enemy
you have no
friends.

GWENDOLYN BROOKS: No Final Words

somewhere between brilliant and genius,
in the neighborhood of great and unforgettable,
as unique wordgiver and kind heart
she emerged as our able witness and deep participant
in a time of unwellness and deep need.
refusing to tap dance with the garbage men of rulership,
corporate acceptance or literary sainthood
she deciphered the multiple layers of accommodation
that often traps the best of us.
she refused first class passage and caviar,
she sidestepped isolation, re-enslavement and tell lies culture.
she remained attached to her language,
her people.
the loss of a mother is a loss of breath.

LANGUAGE
KEEPERS

FIRST WORLD

We were raised on the lower eastside of detroit,
close to harlem, new york, around the block from watts,
next to the mississippi delta in north america.
unaware of source or history, unaware of reasons,
whys or beginnings, accepting tarzan and she-woman,
accepting kong as king, accepting stanley-livingstone and
europecentric africa, accepting british novels, french language
and portuguese folktales that devasted africa's music &
magic, values and vision, people.

you helped restore memories,
gave us place and time,
positioned us within content and warnings,
centered us for the fire from the
first world:
original at dawn, founder of knowledge, inception, definer,
center of life, initial thinker, earliest, earliest order.
primary and wise, foremost, predominantly black explainer,
mature pioneer, seer, roundrooted, earthlike, beginning tree,
cultivator, sourcegiver, genesis, entrance, tomorrow's light.
vision, unarguably african.

for Cheikh Anta Diop

BOOKS AS ANSWER

there was only one book in our home
it was briefly read on Sundays and
in between the lies & promises of smiling men
who slept with their palms out & pants unzipped.
it was known by us children as *the* Sunday book.

rain and books & sun and books to read
in a home where books were as strange as
money and foreign policies discussions
and I alone searched for meaning
where rocks & bells & human storms
disguised themselves as answers, reference and revelation.
and I, a young map of what is missing and wrong
in a home empty of books, void of liberating
words dancing as poetry and song,
vacuous of language that reveals pictures of
one's own fields, spirits, cities and defining ideas.
and I without the quiet meditation that meditative prose
            demands
was left free to drink from the garbage cans of riotous
            imaginations,
was sucked into the poverty of cultural destruction & violent
            answers.
until
someone, a stranger, a dark skinned woman with natural hair,
in a storefront library laid a book in front of me
and the language looked like me, walked like me,
talked to me, pulled me into its rhythms & stares,
slapped me warmly into its consciousness & read,

rain and books & sun and books,
we are each other's words & winds
we are each other's breath & smiles,
we are each other's memories & mores,
we build our stories page by page
chapter by chapter, poem by poem, play by play
to create a life, family, culture & civilization
where it will take more than sixty seconds
to tell strangers who you really are,
to tell enemies and lovers your name.

for Willalyn Fox

SO MANY BOOKS, SO LITTLE TIME

Frequently during my mornings of pain & reflection
when I can't write
or articulate my thoughts
or locate the mindmusic needed
to complete the poems & essays
that are weeks plus days overdue
forcing me to stop, I say cease
answering my phone, eating right, running my miles,
reading my mail and making love.
(Also, this is when my children do not seek me out
because I do not seek them out)
I escape north, to the nearest library or used bookstore.
They are my retreats, my quiet energy/givers, my intellectual
          refuge.

For me it is not bluewater beaches, theme parks
or silent chapels hidden among forest greens.
Not multistored American malls, corporate book
supermarkets, mountain trails or Caribbean hideaways.

My sanctuaries are liberated lighthouses of shelved books,
featuring forgotten poets, unread anthropologists &
playwrights; starring careful anthologists of art & photography,
upstart literary critics, introducing dissertations of tenure-
seeking assistant professors, self-published geniuses, remaindered
first novelists; highlighting speed-written bestsellers,
wise historians & theologians, nobel & pulitzer prize winning
poets & fiction writers, overcertain political commentators,
small press wonderkinds & learned academics.
All are vitamins for my slow brain & sidetracked spirit in this
winter of creating.

I do not believe in smiling politicians, AMA doctors,
zebra-faced bankers, red-jacketed real estate or automobile
salespeople or singing preachers.

I believe in books,
it can be conveniently argued that knowledge,
not that which is condensed or computer packaged but,
pages of hard-fought words, dancing language
meticulously & contemplatively written by the likes of
          me & others,
shelved imperfectly at the levels of open hearts & minds
is preventive medicine strengthening me for the return to my
clear pages of incomplete ideas to be reworked, revised &
written as new worlds and words in all of their subjective
configurations to eventually be processed into books that
will hopefully be placed on the shelves of libraries &
bookstores to be found & browsed over by receptive
booklovers, readers & writers looking for a retreat,
looking for departure & home,
looking for open heart surgery without the knife.

for independent booksellers & librarians: Nichelle Hayes

KEEPING PAPERS ALIVE

books altered the culture of his life,
a DNA effect that transported him southwest
of wherever he was meant to be.
yes, books, journals, magazines and newspapers with
multiple titles, designations and signatures
created in the forms of handwritten prose, typed poetry,
undeciphered african languages, scholar's codes and
playwriter's words, nuances and stage props
all spoke to him in rooms never destined to be his,
small archival spaces amended before he understood the
canons of layered languages rinsed in
garlic & hot sauce mixed with black chocolate, negro bottom ideas
located on that same southeast corner of southwest chi-town.
defending and contemplating memories of woodson, hughes,
wright, brooks, colter, perkins and burroughs—all
engraved permanently, affectionately among peers and others where
readers, scholars and community cluster—
encouraged, given pens and bottles of ink.
reminding us of earlier writers/poets who craved the feel of
black ink to paper creating and exploding ideas, images,
themes, characters and then some to
make our world advance its logical protocols.
you leave prodigious fingerprints.

for Vivian Harsh and on the Retirement of Michael Flug from
The Carter G. Woodson Regional Library of The Chicago Public Library.

LIBRARIES, LIBRARIANS: The Careful Equalizers

they honor the laughter of children
appreciate that it is committed, uninhibited,
innocent and essential in creating wholeness
in the welcoming eyes of our tomorrows   all
thriving on literary nourishment, love and wonderment.

they build spaces that jumpstart and augment our children's
fresh call for colors, light, green avenues, playfulness,
filtered water, large-mindedness, other children, outdoor truths,
cultural sharing, fun, adventure, answers, and clean air.

they are watermelon to their young thirst.

with the book as groundwork, stepladder, and solid stone
anchoring the center place of good thoughts and civilization,
libraries and librarians embrace the public in their name
demanding that the poor, comfortably secure, illiterate, silent questioners
big idea disciples, teachers, new technology carriers, pen & pencil users,
language deciphers, creative culture makers, the quiet and rambunctious,
sacred and secular, reserved and profane,
classroom developers & professors, newspaper
and magazine deadliners, risk takers & slow thinkers,
thesaurus & dictionary collectors, inventors, investors and
beginning scholars
all apprentice in their quest for wisdom, joy, yeses and acceptance.

libraries and librarians in cities, storefronts and no fronts, on rural roads
push forward a mass-based literacy & music
as much of the world discredits
truth sharing. their contemplations are local, urgent and universal in their
advocacy for knowledge as preventive medicine, defining
libraries as anti-ignorance, free, indispensable and authentic.

*for Mary A. Dempsey, Commissioner of Chicago Public Library and for
Librarians worldwide on the occasion of Mary Dempsey receiving the
Chicago Literary Award from the Near South Planning Board's
Harold Washington Literary Award Committee, Friday, June 3, 2011.*

LANGUAGE
CREATORS

TONI

I.
I met you before we met you
before *The Bluest Eye,*
before honors and doubting critics
before the recognition of sisters,
closed eyed brothers reading blank pages of themselves,
faking interest in your stories that
combined an otherworldliness, language-find, answers.

you made sweet cornbread dipped
into soups of complicated Black beans and lives that
only you could recognize, decipher, unpuzzle while
uprooting the superior ignorance of a horribly seasoned people
in the evil cultures, word acceptance and habits of conquerors & whiteness.
for me it was *Sula* and *Beloved* while over-using
Playing in the Dark Africanness.

all directing us to an elevated yes in this time of
slow burn in purgatory of the rich-few and their imitators, and gophers,
who took our bodies and lands and gave us fried-chicken, self-hate, chitterlings,
concrete, blond-haired minds, fake eye-lashes and their god.

II.
it is the artist who questions madness among enemies, lovers,
leaders, friends and family,
it is the artist who does not settle for easy
answers, ineffective conclusions and dirty water,
it is the artist who taught us to rise
above the limiting expectations of others,
loved ones and ourselves,
it is the artist who are the freest people in the world and the
first to warn us of people and a world going mad.

III.
we are the stories we are told,
each creative boundaries in multiple voices.
we answer to names that are not ours,
too many African-Black bodies are buried on foreign soil and
our children are taught by strangers who do not see or
love them.

enter the mountain of tested truths,
enter the raindrops of cleansing wisdom,
enter the valley of right voices,
enter the waves of the blue ocean,
enter the geography of a new commitment,
enter the enlightened heat of Black-Black,
enter the quality of first thought in a world fighting against originality.
enter the beginning rivers of enlightened collaboration with ugliness
seeking the reasons and wellness of Black, Brown and
other hidden languages.

IV.
it is the artists, focused women, a few men
who refuse the comforts of isms, white, Black,
age, sex, class, & other death traps that grew us all.

it is the artist who sees beyond eyesight into
the uncommon fragile bones of the newborn
visualizing possibilities, bright-talk, inspirited learning,
elating smiles, earned anticipation, quiet, shared and informed tomorrows,
knowing deep in their art that a greater future demands family, vision,
historical and cultural emergence, community, sharing elders, living rituals,
accepting the tall shoulders we stand upon and a love-enduring love for
all of nature and the living planet upon which we depend.

it is the artists who take few prisoners in the fight for breaths,
integrity, right-rule, logical laws, clear sounds, music, stories, clear
teachings and trust. all in the service of defeating a spiritual whiteout that
has turned children against children. artists are in the reversal, servicing and
creating business that promotes thinking, contemplation, unknown loves
and yeses.

as you rendered ordinary Black and white folks large and new
missing you is like needing frequent heart-transplants and
early morning breath, among upright aged trees.
we remain vigilant, accordingly Black, culturally & intellectually more and growing.

for Toni Morrison (1931-2019)

BONES

she rifts in less than fifty words
poems that unveil a peoples' bones.

improvising veto-proof likeness
she cleans neighborhoods of celebrated ignorance
among the weak, wicked and wise,
among the wounded, weary and brief winners.

with oxygen lines,
with a vernacular voice and memory
she sings, swims and dances to the merry movements
of the underlooked, bloodflow, heartdrums
and blistered feet of betrayed generations.

this museum of a poet is not about
impressing enemies, friends or lovers,
her urges are to write gladness, grief and melodies.
always probing for trustworthy tales
of her deep-south multitudes.   acutely
aware of the exaggeration of politicians,
public intellectuals and the criminally rich.
she is our brilliant testifier.

for Lucille Clifton (1936-2010)

BLACK EARTH

she was rich memory, melody and best words,
urgent fire riding sun, moon and red dust,
a hat wearing big mama with an iowa ph.d.
Poet of solid songs, cotton fields and Mississippi gumbo,
messenger of our south, Rising.
if truth be liberated, her work navigated the student's spirit in
us.
she left literature, smiles, and ironwood wisdom.
she prepared us to see Black Earth.
daylight at the river's edge always
ready to extinguish square curves and invisible scars.
she was our railroad,
southwind and portrait,
our earth fed tree, soul rooted and able,
clearly a spirited dancer in a land not expecting us to
rise.

for Margaret Walker Alexander (1915-1998)

COURAGE

how does one proceed with half a heart?
what is the message in this transition from
body to spirit to the quiet recesses of our minds,
what should we take from this passing?

there are people who think that their lives are *the* truth.
we walk blindly in the city and the city is all we know
as ignorant people talk about how ignorant other
        people are,
this woman would smile with extended hand and
        heart,
her soul had experienced the white night of loss.

the culturally honest and spiritual among us
are always lied to and laughed at.
in their loneliness they seldom speak
we do not understand them.
we fear their peace and presence,
we fear their questioning the lies in us,
we fear their liberation.

courage is not leaving the battle until the last child is
        accounted for,
courage is saying no to the gossip of fools, friend and foe,
courage is examining the laws and souls of sworn enemies,
courage is creating a life of good values, kindness and small
        deeds.
courage is this woman, Betty Shabazz, daring to cross
the crack in the concrete
drawn by dull-witted prophets who
mistrust the truth of their own god.

for Betty Shabazz (1936-1997)

REMEMBERING BETTY SHABAZZ

i, a poet, a weaver of life, an unfinished soul in motion   still
a closet dancer who greyhounded between
detroit and chicago
on the same roads
that Malcolm Little, Malcolm X, El Hajj Malik El Shabazz
traveled,   the identical highways
that Betty, Betty Shabazz, Dr. Betty Shabazz questioned   still
a poet, an observer of life met Betty,
a giver and nurturer of black winds and earth,
airborne at 33,000 feet over Pennsylvania in the year of 75

i, a poet whose voice was confirmed, layered & enlarged
          after hearing
a "young shining prince," before we knew
we had the sons of kings and queens among us whispering
African truths that gutted the whiteness in our bellies & minds

i, a poet with watered eyes proclaimed cultural love for Black
          memory, future,
family and to Betty Shabazz: a genuine work
in progress devoted to
six plus more of her blood and bones.   still

i, a poet, a weaver of life's tales found a gift at 33,000 feet
a stand for something spirit in st. john knits, sipping vernor's
          ginger ale

a soul in motion electric sliding to the music
of "i'm every woman...
it's all in me," forever observant of predators selling sister love,
          baby love
and a woman's place, a woman's place.   still

i met a woman not a victim,
i met a sister not a tragedy
i met a warrior-teacher not a professional widow,

i met a baobab tree standing permanently against
human hurricanes & earthquakes   still
she was city and voice and insightful storm,
a drop-dead shopper only to give most away,
viewed young people as possibilities, psychic nourishment,
undeveloped innocence mother thoughts   still
she had grown into gianthood
did not fear nameless faces anymore
her prayerful language accented
"hey, girlfriend" or "my brother" burns in our memories   still
peace be still dear Betty
who found the good in us and praised it
I'm every woman, woman, woman,
it's all in me   still.

for Maya Angelou, Ruby Dee, Laura Ross Brown and Susan L. Taylor

ETTA

Etta, not accepting exclusion or
the concept *can't* leaped creatively and courageously into
the 20th century. Her talent, eloquent and grand, evoked
sun, moon, boiling water and well-grain bread. Solid.
she was known to harbor mountains in her heart,
her prodigious artistry conquered the agnosticisms of
minute-minded women and smiling men as lesser souls
buck-danced to the promises of colored stardom. Soon.
Etta at ninety-six is our clear memorandum,
an endearing spirit who took her dreams and songs,
her dance and drama and gracefully grounded a
cultural signature on three generations and a continent.
Solid. As she is.

for Etta Moten Barnett at 96 and Delmarie Cobb

EARTHQUAKES

in the hot of the eye
at the insertion of cayenne
what really matters is:
children catching breath,
children experiencing love and continuation.
children understanding the good and emerging evil,
children expecting a future,
children smiling quickly and uninhibited
in this world.
        as the smiles cease conflict beckons
        hearts hurt   blood rushes   hands sweat
        pain ensues and comes like pins in the spine
understand this:
conscious men do not make excuses
do not expect their women to carry their water,
harvest the food and prepare it too.
world over it is known that
breast sucking is only guaranteed to babies.
        sisters if the men do not fight,
        if the men are not responsible
cover the breast   close the legs   stop the love
cancel good times   erase privileges   question manhood.

if the men engage the enemy
get ready for rumor & divisive headaches
everyone will want to know their price,
traitors will try & confirm that the men can be
        bought,
enemies will pass gold to family & lovers to buy his
        dreams.
if the engaged men are of the wise kind
they will appreciate the greater needs and
without doubt or hesitation tell them our pay back is:
georgia, the states of florida & alabama, we want
texas.

when the smiles quit when the laughter quiets
conflict beckons   hearts hurt   blood rushes
        hands sweat
spines strengthen   & brothers comprehend.
catch the sun & get on up
rise on the run. open eyed
ready & expecting danger

expecting earthquakes.

for Frances Cress Welsing (1935-2016)

MARGARET BURROUGHS, HAKI R. MADHUBUTI AND CHARLIE BURROUGHS
(20th anniversary celebration of Third World Press in 1987)

MASTER OF COLORS AND CANVAS

how did we arrive?
mothers as artists and seers
as earth toilers, sun consumers
workers at midnight and dawn
nurtured us with apples, bananas, open hearts, seeds,
cultural language, illustration and institutions.
lovingly cut the umbilical cord,
not the commitment or sacred findings.

you with the brushes, canvas, paint, tools and ideas
with African hair, mind and memory
instigated an uprising to change the conversation
quickening our run toward saneness, smiles and fear
out-pacing a leadership who moves
like roaches with alzheimers.

today,
we, on jet powered roller skates
still eat your dust
still are wondrous of the measure
of your gifts.

for Dr. Margaret Burroughs, July 12, 2008

Photo courtesy of Bok-Keem Bolo Nyerere (6-19-98)

GWENDOLYN BROOKS, HAKI R. MADHUBUTI AND SONIA SANCHEZ

ART III SONIA SANCHEZ: Drawing Fire

we were so young born into a storm
searchers in the spirit of all that was good, just, correct and
immediately right surely possible accenting Black & African.
in the historical western theatre of hidden truths, gigantic lies
of past precious seconds raging into days, months, years,
centuries always in the necessary acts of seeking that
which brings meaning, memory & answered solutions of Black & Blackness
issues in laughter, defines beauty neutralizing and encompasses ugly that
initiates work that encourages families within families   Black
always claiming art as the starting point of our unique journey
not yet finished as we put foot in front of foot   Black
circling ideas of resistance, liberation & mama's peach cobblers.
as we confront fear, anger, each other & the world as the
state houses, death squads & traders stole our youth, mothers and fathers
we were so young   dodging hurricanes
entering the sixties & seventies of the last century
as soldiers and youth committed to the groundwork beginning of the
Black Arts Movement   BAM

art, artists, the image makers, storytellers who visualized the
best & worst of the human condition is what is missing all too much
in today's complicated arena of "what do you do?"   BAM

poet, "how you gonna make a living?"
by joining the word creators, the smile makers,
the happy hands, feet movers, doubt catchers
    sub/surface explorers, idea incubators
the look you in the eye/say/yes people.
where are today's impossible task takers?
the 24/7 bush women, men & young people living on promises,
coffee, the breath of lies, bad food, tea, each other, and the
wonderment of discovery from the Black Arts Movement of fire to
the Hip Hop Movement of rain without sunshine, moon or the underside
of heat & mud, you recognized and called the young to conference
to listen as they rapped the underside of ugly teaching them to never forget
mamas, sisters, grandmamas revealed that

stopping the women stops the future
ha ha
stopping the women stops the future
ha ha ha
we stood on the shoulder of houston, wright, mckay, toomer,
tolson, danner, fanon, hayden, du bois, robeson, locke, brown, cullen,
garvey, washington, douglass, wheatley, dunbar, woodson, wells-barnett,
    and the drowned voices of a people becoming whole.
in the mid-sixties of the last century   running
of a millennium that raped us from a continent we began to gain a voice
    running
as malcolm (el-hajj malik el-shabazz) and many planted their seeds &
    initiated a hurricane
that hit america and changed the course of the sun:
gwendolyn brooks, margaret walker, dudley randall, mari evans, sara webster fabio
amiri & amini baraka, broadside press, negro digest/black world, jayne
cortez, motown,
don l. lee, sweet honey in the rock, larry neal, civil rights black power movements,
journal of black poetry, askia toure, soul book, liberator, marvin x, eugene
redmond, the philadelphia sound, kalamu ya salaam, sekou toure, third world
press, nikki giovanni, black books bulletin, audre lorde, carolyn rodgers, obac,
sterling plump, hoyt w. fuller, john oliver killens, nation of islam, james bald-
win, ossie davis, ruby dee, sun ra, harry belafonte, coltrane, nina simone, ted
joans, max roach, abby lincoln, johari amini, joe goncalves & martin luther king jr.

sonia sanchez, sister sonia on the road always crossing borders and cultures as
the blue black narrator haunted by injustice   running
chanting her syllables exploring the limits of language of
what is not said, said and undersaid taking the margins of life
away from fear filled backrooms and lynching trees
always the outsider creating loud peripheries,
a first responder, as in how do we recapture
hundreds of years of who we once were,
how to jumpstart the minds, bodies, souls
of the internet, facebook & twitter generation
as to make the world right for morani and mungu and for all the children born
with "you can't" in their eyes believing good health and wealth is for the other.
avoiding pigfeet, chitlins, sucking on bones and

the lies of the cow's milk enthusiasts,
if it has a face she will not eat it
if it runs from her it will not be cooked,

if she has to chase food, it will not be caught or consumed,
her rice is brown, her vegetables rooted green and green,
her fruit consumed at the peak of ripeness,
her water double filtered with a touch of lemon,
her juices fresh and slowly ingested like vitamins to organs
her shadow speaks emancipation, clarity and resistance
her voice is south african click songs

in her solitude her utterances are never anonymous
we both still believe in handwriting, note taking &
book reading page by page by page.

sonia is 100 pounds of wet raw energy
body language in words   huh
pulled from the underside of now   huh huh BAM
spitting razor blade lyrics against euro-whites edges bent
on silencing the heroic and sheroic voices who dared question white
lightening supremacy, and our self-hatred boils in rat's blood disguised
as johnny walker red and kool-aid.
it is the artist of all cultures, in all of their many configurations who
catch breath, running, missed meals, baths & teeth brushing   running
who bent metal, blended colors, escalated love of self and others,
running lived shared lives, blows horns, beat drums   running
encouraged dancing feet and core running withstood criticism, internal-
ized water as in
river, sea, and ocean running often land locked,
between gifted and genius   always running
against doubt, ignorance and deep poverty   running

luminous in her ability to absorb the earth's gifts and trumpet players
running
blowing unknown territories running and running whose colors
capture meaning, acute imagination and the ever present
questions of sound and sane memory running running

giving us a poet of clear guidance and off, off rhymes, haikus and
full moon of sonia
never to trip into despair or irrelevancy   running   running
go tell that.
awoman, awoman, awoman

MAGNIFICENT TOMORROWS

1.
flames from sun
fire in during rainbow nights.

the women are colors of earth and ocean—
earth as life,
the beginning waters,
magnificent energy.

as the women go, so go the people,
determining mission,
determining possibilities.

stopping the women stops the future.
to understand slavery, feel the eyes of mothers.
there lies hope even in destruction, lies unspeakable horror or
fruitful destiny.

we
are now in the europe of our song,
non-melody with little beat or hope,
current dreams are visionless,
producing behavior absent of greatness.

2.
without great teachings,
without important thoughts,
without significant deeds,
the ordinary emerges as accepted example
gluing the women
to kitchens,
afternoon soaps
and the limiting imagination of sightless men.
producing
a people that move with the
quickness of decapitated bodies

while
calling such movement
divine.

possibilities: listen to the wind of women, the voices of big
mama, zora neale, sister rosa, fanny lou, pretty renee, gwen
brooks, queen nzinga and warrior mothers, all birth and
prophecy, Black and heart warm, bare and precise, the women
detailing the coming collapse or rise, the best and bent of youth
emerging, telling triumphantly, if we listen, if we feel & prepare.

3.
if black women do not love,
there is no love.
if black women do not love,
harmony and sustaining humanity cease.
if black women do not love,
strength disconnects.
families sicken, growth is questionable &
there are few reasons to conquer ideas or foe.

as black women do not love,
europe gives way to southern meals.
as black women mature,
so come flames from sun,
rainbows at dusk.
sculpture of elizabeth catlett and
music of nina simone.
as women black connect,
the earth expands, minds open and books reveal the possible
if we study
if we feel the flow & secrets of our women,
if we listen,
if we concentrate,
if we carefully care,
if we simply do.

for Queen Mother Moore, Karima White, Sonia Sanchez, Mari Evans,
Ruby Dee, Assata Shakur, Julia Fields and Janet Sankey

THE SEA IN YOUR LANGUAGE

She came to Urbana loving literature
stayed to start a movement among wheat, soybeans & vacant
    smiles
words always precede battle and battery
    even where the language is not broken, torn or wanting.
Amidst the English-English you do not disappoint.
Revelation: it's rough being a woman, Black, slim, immaculate
with a brain as quick as fire in their tongue and ours.

Radical surgery allowed you to walk away from fear
making you incapable of treachery or grinning rhetoric.
Words matter. Some cut like big Willie's razor, bloodless.
others come deceptively like Vietnamese art, long history, short
    notice.
twenty years of working in white shadows
qualifies you for a double zero preceding your name.
your memory is of banished bones and promises.

Did I say she is the sea in you and me, and
morning tulips, red spirits, rainbow colors. Wow!
Our kind of woman. Running buddy. Sister. Genuine.
Announce her as valuable earth, hatwearer with a killer smile.

for Sandra Gibbs, November 20, 1999

MAMA ANN FOREVER

hmmmm   bop,   hmmmm   bop.   bop
hmmmmmm,   hmmmm
bop   remember this   bop   lost minds rising
one death can't stop the music
can't stop the righteous language of song
within the song of songs
of dance created and inspired by songs & ancestors
step,   step,   step   angalia watoto
can't stop the music   bop
can't stop the mamas who can't be bought
with popcorn promises of fame and new enslavement
can't stop the mamas and babas of laughter and rhythm
who love children,   hmmmmmmmm   loved our children
who loved the celebration of teaching the children
notes upon notes upon magical beats to the inner brain
got this, she got this   bop
dance with the what,   what about forgotten tomorrows
the children Black,   deep Black & Brown,   yellow-Black,
off Black,   want to be Black   want to be African
color them with the language and the culture of a
misused people,   of a raped people   recovering from PTSD
who you is TJ,   pants below the crack in yo mind?
who you is pretty shanica   thinking beauty will get you the world?
who you is willie-joe   guns in each hand claiming
Black corners of little value owned by others   hating yo Black self,
hating Black people   and all you were *taught to* hate
in a nation of "for sale Negroes" dancing to the message of europe & whiteness
who sold our music to the unpeople who kidnapped a continent,
seasoned our minds,   bodies and spirits   but
couldn't stop the Black-African music,   the dance,   the offbeat drums
the live beating bass,   the in-between play of sax and trumpet
of piano and voice of big bands and sextets
playin nina, train, monk, ellington & ella,
playin pops, sarah, dolphy, & the arts ensemble of chicago
not running from blakey, silvers, pharaoh, shepp, max,
in and out of the tradition of the AACM

culture in the luminous and right keys
to stop maniacs and trumps, to side kick the false dozens
disguised as democracy and homecomings of white-collared leaders singing the
spirituals – blues of belgium, of texas, of attica, the Hamptons and
midtown manhattan.
and there is *Mama Ann* at midnight and dawn
Mama Ann at first-light, with fresh water-falls of
unquenched will and musical wealth.
she was our connective left-hand with a mean melody right
guiding our children into the wisdom of music
this is no game, no false beginnings or ending
it is they, the nouns and adjectives of our scattered minds, disjointed
commas,   periods,   stories,   stanzas,   bars and   recovering memory of
"dance to the music"
who is in charge here, there, everywhere and else?
who writes the checks in this house?
or is it like pharaoh who only took cash before he blew.
ours is a fight against gigantic ugly,
ours is a quest to recall tradition, first needs and words,
ours is a mini foundation of music, a dominance & rainbows,
of lester's hats, billie's flowers, and bird's fingers
combining the fundamentals of a clear conscious of
i know why i'm here!
i know the mission of the gifted and the anointed,
i know the place of beauty, harmony, culture and money,
& money played in the mind-taking of a people—
i know who i am,   why i am *here*
alive among the Black offspring, the bright-eyed youth
of an indomitable people rising, *betrayal ends here*!
betrayed as the devil's mission stops here!
they call me Mama Ann
and that is, and they are who i am
remember my name,
remember my calling,
remember my instrument and the melodies of a life
well played. *hmmmmmmm*
hmmmmmmm bop, hmmmmmmm bop, *bop*

for Mama Ann Ward (1949-2016)

63

"Laborers in the fields of the Arts."
—Ossie Davis
"I call myself a reader and I don't
want reading to go out of style."
—Ruby Dee

there is calmness here
on the stage belonging to dramatists, applause and history
to dark colors in their affirmation of yes and yes,
early footsteps on the pavement of injustice and art,
in the languages of black, brown, Yiddish and other,
laboring two for one at minimum wage
in the gut-wrenching absence of homegrown narratives
challenged by a people with slow feet, sore hands,
steel spines, missing teeth and unrecorded memories
claiming the children of all cultures and breaths,
addressing endlessly the exhaustion of race; confirming
we'll make our world within this world.

art cures ignorance, boredom and one good nerve,
never too abundant to share,
less the center but is central,
a bearer of intellect, caring and talent,
views all children as children as children
as luminous souls in sacred skins and laughter.

there is calmness   hear?
among the blacklisted, whitelisted and no listed,
fearless, royal, coupled and loved: our first family
aglow at dusk and warm soup,
defying the iced veins banishing weapons,
first to take the bullets,
but seldom failing to fire back,
she remains our answer before the questions.

for Ruby Dee (1922-2014)

YELLOW**BLACK**

HELEN MAXINE GRAVES LEE
1945

MAXINE AND JIMMY LEE

My mother loved my father.
He took her virginity and gave her me.
Her love for him was life-changing and life-
determining. She never loved again.
She said it was too painful.
Her beauty attracted oceans of men from all
cultures. Few men could really handle the way
she looked. Men of wealth, influence and
potential proposed to her.
She never married again.
She said that love is a beautiful concept but not
for women like her. Men wanted to lock up her
beauty. They did not trust themselves and
refused to trust her. She said the hearts of most
men were corrupted in the act of becoming
men. She chose to be alone with her children
and memories of southern sunlight.
It was clear to her, no one was
going to take care of us, but us.

MAXINE

My mother was the color of papaya and
bananas, her smile could weaken the strongest
of men. She was uncommonly beautiful.
Her face and body forced men to forget so
called social etiquette. They all, upon seeing
her, would dream for a moment.

Many men, married, single and committed,
old, young, saints, sinners and in-between
wanted a chance with Helen Maxine Graves.
Most men were willing to risk everything to
taste the flesh of a fourteen-year-old girl in a
woman's body who had no idea that her beauty
would define her life and that of her children.
Jimmy Lee got the first hit, with his smile,
music, lies, sexual know-how and promises.
She ceased looking at other boys or men.
This was her first mistake.

HELEN MAXINE

My mother was so beautiful that she not only stopped
cars, she stopped buses.
Her beauty, if just for a moment, made most men's
eyes roam and forget other women.
She was music unemployed.
She wrapped her body in clothes that refused to hide
the nature of her desires.
She wanted to be a dancer.
She wanted to be warm weather year-round.
She wanted to know the origin of walnuts and wealth.
She wanted to play the harmonica
and sing like Billie Holiday. She believed in God, kind
Negroes, reciprocity and
southern food. Her clothes got in the way of men
taking them off.

.

HELEN MAXINE: Two

Once I accidentally walked in on my mother
and a customer having sex, she was covered by
his body. I, at an early age, knew that she was
working. I saw no enjoyment in her eyes, heard
few cries of real pleasure or endearment.
In the room I shared with my sister, where
I was always instructed to go when she was
working, I consumed Black literature and
dreamed of better days. I soon realized that sex
was also an empowering tool for beautiful
women who, like professional athletes, had less
than a ten year window to make it or find
another trade.

My mother, in her 34th year, four years on the
other side of men lining up for favors and six
years into the bottle and needle, ended up
cleaning houses for white folks in-between the
weekends of lost memory, sagging body and

unending cries of a lost life. Seeing her like that
tore my young heart apart, flawed my perception
of the world and helped determine my decisions
and lifestyle. I never drank alcoholic
liquors, never been high, never smoked.
I viewed drunkenness as a weakness and a curse
on our people. Without knowing it, at 14, I was
searching for a healthy lifestyle and eventually
I was to find it in the literature I consumed.

HELEN MAXINE: Three

The beginning of my mother's end was when
she could not start her day without a drink.
Quickly that drink was followed by another and
another until her body shut down.

I would seek out her hiding places for alcohol
and drugs and destroy them. She would leave
the house on Fridays and often didn't return
until Sunday night or Monday morning. Often,
I would search the local hotels and homes with
rooms to let, seeking her out. I remember my
many fights with strange men who had paid for
a night or weekend and cared little about a son
trying to protect his mother.

I, at 6'1", 131 pounds, did not inject too much
fear in the hearts of men much larger than me.
This was my advantage: I carried a lead pipe in
my belt and could use it and the language of

the streets with a righteous certainly that
would force most men to stand down before
confrontation.
I was ready and willing to fight for Helen Maxine
Graves Lee—I was all she had.
And that was clearly not enough.

HELEN MAXINE: The Last Conversation

The last conversation my mother and I had was
a fight. I had bought two new shirts to wear for
special occasions at school. I was an A student
and frequently called upon to represent my class
or the school in academic or musical contests
and presentations. The morning of a major
event I could not find one of my shirts.
My mother had worn it the night before
and was fast asleep in it.
I couldn't control my anger and
brought her to tears with my hurt and utter
dissatisfaction of my life, her life,
my sister's life and our general existence.
Within a week she was dead.

MAKING TRANSITIONS

My mother never recovered from the many noises in her life. What I remember of her going home ritual is that complete strangers said nice things about her and the casket was not open. I wore my first brand new suit without a tie, sitting in the front row with family members I did not know. I could not cry. My sister, with a new baby in her arms, did not dry her eyes for a week. I was on my own. My sister and her baby were on their own and we didn't have a security or escape net. She went to my grandfather's church and home for help. I didn't. a family member asked why I stopped going to church. I said that it "affected my relationship with God." That next week I was on a Greyhound bus to Chicago. I was seventeen, on my own, going to seek help from a stranger—my father.

FOR HELEN MAXINE GRAVES LEE

Helen Maxine Graves Lee was here.
Her son knew it, her daughter loved it.
There wasn't a terrible artery to her heart
her blood flow was warm and ancient
accenting her human kindness and mercy
which translated among the urban walkers
as weakness, naivete and fragile weather.

She loved God.
She loved the men of God.
Through him and them she searched
and reached for salvation.
They populated her bed and head,
pleasured themselves, moved in and out of
her life like a Los Angeles rush hour
in the heat of hot sex.
She lost her God.
The men of God only noticed
her weight gain and less frequent smiles

as she accepted their pennies and criticism
without comment or eye contact.

Her's was a pure heart,
her son knew it,
her daughter learned it,
the men of God continued on their way
finding newer and younger
Helen Maxine Graves Lees.

HEARTLOVE

MAINTAINING LOVESHIPS

There are many paragraphs in a life of love. I say "paragraph" because the stanza of poetry is still foreign to most of us. Love is a living river running slowly north to south, traversing the entire human continent. Love is like the Mississippi River experiencing all types of weather, hot to cold, warm to cool, frigid to steaming hot. Find the weather of the person you love, monitor it often. Or like the river's weather, adjust your body temperatures to accommodate the other in your life and adapt to your own definitions of happiness, stability, and seriousness. Remember that love is not a swimming contest, and most of us will never learn to backstroke. Learn to swim upstream together.

Bonding—mating, and preferably marriage to another—is or can be music. (Much of the time, in this culture, it is regrettable noise.) However, this bonding can be the best of the early Supremes, Miracles, Four Tops and Nat King Cole. Some of us, measured our early happiness with each new cut by the Dells.

"Stay in My Corner." Coupling is also Bessie Smith, Billie Holiday and, yes, Nina Simone—as they sing with tears in their eyes, "Am I Blue?" We choose our dancing partners. We can either two-step, tap, do modern, African, the breakdown, or get in line and pulse. Whatever tune we choose will demand work, require navigating the personal river of the other, require the sharing of the most intimate spaces. We may be southern in our spirit, yet, too often, our struggle is to neutralize the northern winds blowing ice into our lives. Think in bright possibilities.

A BONDING

we were forest people.
landrooted. vegetable strong.
feet fastened to soil with earth strengthened toes.
determined fruit,
anchored
where music soared,
where dancers circled,
where writers sang.
where griots gave memory,
where smiles were not bought.

you have come to each other in wilderness,
in this time of cracked concrete, diminished vision, wounded
          rain.
at the center of flowers your craft is on fire.
only ask for what you can give.

do not forget bright mornings, hands touching under moonlight,
filtered water for your plants, healing laughter, renewing
futures. caring.

your search has been rewarded, marriage is not logical, it's necessary.
we have a way of running yellow lights, it is now
that we must claim
the sun in our hearts. your joining is a mending, a quilt.

as determined fruit
you have come late to this music,
only ask for what you can give.
you have asked for each other.

for Susan and Khephra, August 20, 1989

QUIET MOUNTAINS TO YOUR ELEGANCE

Yours is a regenerative descent.

This community has witnessed your maturation,
this community has participated in the birth and
nurturing of your child,
this community has embraced your design,
this community has grown in the glow of your
        commitment.

Now that you have chosen to rejoice
in this quarter century of your love
we too renew our song.

We grow quiet mountains to your elegance.
yours are right memory, precious culture,
intricate calling, bonding,
affirming the Africa reach in us.
The exactness of your love replenishes the drumbeat in
        our steps.
Come as calm weather, muted in the understanding
that within decades of tumultuous stirrings
your melody is original antique,
determined answering, a smile.

Let this be our legacy,
our melody.

for Carolyn and Charles on 25 years of marriage, September 19, 1993

CONTEMPLATING FULL ORCHARDS

New York City is not a place to watch
the sun or grow a forest, agreed.

I speak from the tongue of a father,
a brother, as one who has known deep love.

This marriage is not an exam. You are now
entering the rooms of living mysteries where
prophesy reveals itself as knowledge and mother-wit.
This is the clearest contingency for love:
        commitment to differences, listening, compromise.
        assigned prescriptive silences,
        learned laughter, artful music and essential values.

In fresh marriages you are exposed
like new seeds in earth,
like delinquent gossip from children,
like well water to the earth's organisms.
define your memories gracefully.

Sweet, sweet lovers
crowd your bed in each other.
rise each day with distinctive voices
contemplating full orchards draped in
bountiful moons of mastered touching.
Accepting the unpredictable,
expecting well-placed joy. Agreed.

for Bakari Kitwana and Monique Jacques, November 26, 1995

BREATHING THE BREADTH OF THE OTHER

same love different decades.
we've seen the sun
rise
melting loud promises of our twenties.
the young do not love carefully,
the young innocently love, often,
the young *live* with wishes of no boredom.

you are mature young
a decade past romanticism,
years on the other side of searching,
months away from intimate hunger,
weeks from assigning blame,
days removed from contemplating advice from
    relatives,
within seconds confirming, we are ready!

these are your commitments:

a. listen first, listen last, communicate.
b. when angry, hit the couch in private instead of each other.
   measure each other's pulse seven times a week; do
   not buy a pulse meter.
c. divide the housework.
       B.C. (Before Children)
       he: garbage, dishes, bedroom, car, kitchen,
          mopping weekly wash, cooking, shopping,
          no pets.
she: living room, bathroom, halls, cooking, car,
    sweeping, shopping, weekly wash, kitchen,
    argue for a cat.

A.C. (After Children) revise everything
d. encourage growth in each other. intelligence may
marry stupid, but brains don't stay with pinheads.
e. parent against the culture; if you spend $100 on
nintendo, your children will become what you deserve.
f. do not take current beauty for granted. big eaters
are wrong.
g. grow into greater love, nothing stays the same.
challenge the beauty in each other. fight for
understanding.

we've seen the sun
rise
in you
knowing the bones in her back,
feeling the tenderness of his feet,

same love, different decade,
breathing the scent of each other
breath to breath
sustaining the music of bright expectations
life confirmed. complete.
one.

for Lynn and Ron Rochon, August 22, 1993

DARKROOTED: The Joining

It is said each morning before parting, before meeting
the wind, the two of you clasp sun-touched hands &
sing a quiet prayer for the continued wholeness & safety
of the other. Anchoring. It is known that your four hands
touching softly complete the first circle, mending
the two of you quilt-like into an unending image of
        long-distances
earth trees, in this kente-cloth man who is brother to
his community lies deep well values, wind-swept valleys.
mountains, broad memory, historical pain, committed
joy, energy, determined force. I've seen his father.
In this batik-cloth woman whose beauty graced our eyes
there is crystal-hope. Renewing grass spirit, watered fruit,
heartbeat cook, active brain, willing searcher.
serious runner. I've seen the people of her homeland.
we listen to the sunlight burning between your hearts.
we confirm the enchanted beat of your calling.
as in water conversing with sea rocks we come
        touch-tongue,
we come joyfully to your circle,
Duplicating the quest, you are yes, anchored african trees.
darkrooted. Ones.

for Marilyn and David Hall, June 23, 1990

THE UNION OF TWO

what matters is the renewing and long running kinship
seeking common mission, willing work, memory, melody, song.

marriage is an art,
created by the serious, enjoyed by the mature,
watered with morning and evening promises.

those who grow into love
remain anchored
like egyptian architecture and seasonal flowers.

it is african that woman and man join in smile, tears, future.
it is traditional that men and women share expectations,
       celebrations, struggles.
it is legend that the nations start in the family.
it is african that our circle expands.
it is wise that we believe in tomorrows, children, quality.
it is written that our vision will equal the promise.

so that your nation will live and tell your stories accurately,
you must be endless in your loving touch of each other,
your unification is the message,
continuance the answer.

for Ife and Jake, August 7, 1986

ANSWERS: This Magic Moment

now that you have young love
insist upon the dawn,
its mornings bright with sun and rain
that summon up continuity.

now that your love is bonded and
culturally confirmed, do not forget:
first meetings, great and early laughter,
preparation for first dates, delicate touches and
kisses that quicken heartbeats, love notes and
phone calls into the midnights' dawns. do not forget
promises; there are always pure promises of,
        "forever yours."

now that you are one and one. matched.
remember the path that joined you.

now that you have traditional clarity and
are blessed with conscientious givers among you,
do not forget world without light or hope,
do not forget brutality, hunger, raw violence
visited upon children.

share the beauty in your eyes this day,
grow into mature love, leaving little for granted.

insist upon the dawn,
its mornings bright with sun and rain,
summoning rainbows and continuity,
summoning you here, brilliantly beautiful,
caring, content, young lovers,
growing into your promises,
confirming life,
confirming us,
giving an answer.

for Gina and Chester, August 18, 1990

TURNING TOWARD JOY

it is the goodness in these anointed souls,
two middle-love wonderments supplying breath to the other
mastering art, silence, political slaps and wondrous music.
whole voices are heard in the midst of double joy.
come quiet, come smiling, come as assured lovers
in Barbados summer's January for this joining.

millet, flowers, ripe fruit and tenderness surround r & r.
in a decade of terror & danger they protect each other's heart.
they are bookends, palm trees, Brooklyn stop signs & bone true,
not islands, their love is a continent of perceptive rivers feeding lakes
among clean wishes and whispers tuning our ears southward.

absolutely acknowledging sacred learning and spiritual answers,
declaring permanent inquiries of we've arrived,
you, together, taste the juice, water & bread of each other's delicate touch.
clear perfection confirms africa and the diaspora,
honors tradition, family, ancestors and future.

your melody is enlightened oxygen summoning life, promises and yes.

you share breath.

for Rashida Irene Bumbray and Rashid Kwame Shabazz, January 15, 2011

WOMEN BLACK: Why These Poems

to see her is to realize why man was made different. is to realize why men were cut rough & unready & unfinished. the contrast would be like a magnet, and we fell into each other like wind with storm, like water into waiting earth. this woman black, this unbelievable wonder, would test the authenticity of a man's rough, a rap of beautifully rhymed words would not work with her. a well-rehearsed smile on the good side of your face or that special gleam from under your tanned shades could not penetrate this woman black. even the whole of you, in your pants tight with life, did not cause undo motion in her.

woman means more than *woman*
more than brown thighs
black lips, quick hips &
unfounded rumors
more than the common, more than the rational & irrational,
more than music, more than rough stones & unread books,
more than keepers of the kitchen, more than berry black,
mellow yellow & town brown, more than quick pussy, more than european
names followed by degrees, more than nine to five order takers, more than
fine, more than fox evil eyes big legs tight hips or women of the summer.

this is why i write about you. i want to know you better. closer, so this is my message to you. not a study. not a judgement or verdict. just observations and experiences. a lifestory, specifically the last fifty years. above all poems of love going against that which is mistakenly passed off as *love*. this is a collection of intense feeling and complete touch. these are poems that were not ripe or ready for earlier books. these are poems that had to come to you in their own time, their own color & meaning. i have tried to do you justice in all of my works, but this Woman of the Sun, is the real test of my seriousness & dedication to you. my mother & her mother are here, my father's mother is here, my sister is here, the women Black that i have loved & loved & loved & still love are here. my wife, quietly, as is her way, travels throughout these pages. this is the work that i slept, ate and traveled with. this is the beginning & middle the overtouched, with memories from arkansas to michigan to illinois. this is an inadequate gift to the other half of me, and to the whole of you. the you that often goes unnoticed, unheard & unthanked. the you that is lost is in the power plays of men and life.

LOVEPOEMS

1.
lately
your words are drugged passages
with razor edges
that draw blood & tears
      and
memories of less difficult moments
when   love
that beautiful   overused   emotion-packed commitment
charged the body.
love
momentarily existed
actually transformed us defying the odds
flourishing   enlarging us
if only for seconds
seconds that were urgently expected
and
overneeded.

2.
there are rumors afloat that love
is ill.
intimacy at best is overnight
clashes
and morning regrets.
are
bodies underwashed in strange bathrooms
as lovers
& others   bang the door
softly running.
steppin cautiously in cracked silence
to spread rumors   that
love
is a diseased bitch
deserving death and quick
cremation.

3.
do not wait to be loved
seek it,
the unexplainable
fight for love
not knowing whether you have
lost or accomplished
poetic possibilities
dig deep for love
search while acknowledging
the complexity of the heart & fading standards.
in seeking love use care.
to let a stranger come into you
too quickly
may make you a stranger to yourself.

4.
from dawn to dusk in cities
that sunrises often fail to visit

we imprisoned light
& generated heat.

you are seedless grapes and
bright stars at winter & wind.
there are voices in your smiles
and confirmation in the parting of your lips.

SAFISHA

1.
our joining into one proceeded like
sand through a needle's eye.
slow, bursting for enlargement & uncertainty.
a smoothing of passion and ideas
into spirited permanence and love.

there are decades of caring in you,
children loving that makes the father
in me active and responsible.
you forecasted the decline of marble shooting
& yo yo tricks, knowing too that hopscotch
& double dutch could retard early minds if
not balanced with challenges and language.

you are what brothers talk about
when serious & committed to loving life.
when examples are used to capture dreams
you are that woman.
for me you are summer at midlife,
daring spirit and middlenoon love
and the reason I return.

2.
dark women are music
some complicated well-worked
rhythms
others   simple melodies.
you are like soft piano
black keys dancing between
& not becoming the white.
you bring dance & vision into our lives.
it is good & good
to be your
man.

WOMENBLACK: We Begin With You

our women we begin with you
black, beige, brown, yellowblack and
darkearth we dropped from your womb
in joyscreams lifegiver
you're worlds apart from the rest.

our women
imagine a warm breeze in any city
in the west that will not choke you,
be wife, be mother, a worker or professional
maker you still my lady.
our women
of fruits & vegetables
of greens & color   of sounds & potholes
of mountains & earth clearing danger   from
doorways who did not ruin their teeth & bodies
with the blood of pigs & cattle or fried chicken
after stumpin at bob's place till five in the daylight.
partyin was almost like a job
in motion on the run we are the rhythm people.

womenblack
unusual maker you say,
fine as all getout you say,
finer than lemonade in the shade,
we are a part of you maker, woman of
the autumn earth mother of sunlight
& I seldom say "I love you"
love is not our word. love belongs to
soap operas & comic books, is the
true confessions of the pale people from
the winter's cold.
we are the people of motion, move on motion
dance on, summer, summer lady.

womenblack we care about you
a deep & uncontrollable penetrative
care   as we listen to our own hearts,
whatever the weather.
you don't have to build a pyramid
in order to be one & you are still my
maker rhythm, rhythm lady.

our women we begin with you
black, beige, brown, yellowblack and
darkearth we dropped from your womb
in joyscreams lifegiver
you're worlds apart from the best.
you are in me and I in you
deep
deep and endless forever
touch to touch,
end to beginning
until the stars kiss the earth
and
our music will be songs of liberation.

for Safisha

RAINFOREST

you are forest   rain
dense with life green colors
forever pulling the blue of life into you
see you walk and
i would like to burst rainwater into you
swim in & out of you
opening you like anxious earthquakes
uncontrollable but beautiful & dangerous.

get with this woman   come
fire frozen beauty,
men cannot sleep around you
your presence demands attention
demands notice
demands touch & motion & communication.

you are runner
swift like warm wind hurricanes
fast like stolen firebirds
& you disrupt the silence in me
make me speak memories long forgotten & unshared.
secrets uttered in strange storms,
deep full sounds reserved for magical,
magical lovers.

listen runner
i have shared pain with you,
i have commented on future worlds to you,
i have let you touch the weak & strong of me,
i have tasted the tip of your ripeness &
kissed sweat from your middle.
i have bit into your mouth & sucked the lifeforces from yr insides   and
i know you. understand you.
i have shared books & travel & music & growth with you.

sweet knows honey & I know you.
under salted water tides
& running against polluted earth
i've tried to be good to you woman
tried to care beyond words
            care beyond distant spaces
sensitive phases & quiet lies
care
beyond cruel music & false images.

you are original high & dream maker
& true men do not try to limit you.

listen woman black
I do not wish to dominate your dreams
or obstruct your vision.
trust my motion   feel
know that I am near and with you
& will cut the cold of winter winds to reach you.
you are delicate bronze
in spring-summers and special autumns
you are forest rain
dark & runner & hurricane-black
frequently
I say frequently I bring you
midnight   *rain.*

THE ANSWER

when did they begin to sing together? what tunes grounded their hearts into one, joined their smiles, quieted each other's criticisms of the other and found them becoming the period in each other's sentences? name the hard winter, warm morning, human and animal centered river that flows between them. sounds like deep grass, uncut string beans, sautéed broccoli occasioned with the protein of underwater life-forms that nourishes them and the earth's people. she is book and history, he, music and tech, both nurtured in the Black-african-panamanian rhythms of long lineage people. quilted. they are the last of their family's 20th century deep tree births, representing moon, sun, connecting continents, memory, spirit and focused struggles. I got this. love conquers languages, finds answers in the unsaid, slow bones of this hip hop nomad who communicates in catch-lines and humor, with a body that could hide behind a toothpick. she, as teacher, cleared the right moments for analysis that trapped a part of his heart that only she knew existed; her beauty does matter, it is luminous and sticks like post-it notes with their future written in long hand. we got this. their parents as participant world-knowers, travelers who met at the a-woman/a-man corner of yes, to welcome their children to yesteryears, the present, tomorrow and quiet-as-it-is kept, family personified and layered, always questioning and forever growing. it is tradition.

.

for Akili Malcolm Lee and Janeen Panisha Waller on
the occasion in their union, July 3, 2011

CULTURAL DAUGHTER

the common language between us is art and family. You are exemplary in the millet rice and wheat fields of the talented, magnificent in music, are able to bend a note to the curve in your ear, hear melodies and chords throughout morning time & at midnight, are fluent in the alphabet of questioning the flats, angles and shapes of high rhythm. You came to us over twenty years ago, in short-shorts on a Saturday afternoon, looking for answers and work. Your willingness willed a presence that foretold the impact that night/day study, 24/7 practicing, quick called rehearsals, around the clock composing, fighting the male ego, confronting musical patriarchs and all that goes with a company of brilliant women declaring no to the backseat of come-get-this. It was a yes in your flutes, a confirmation of your daughter's needs, always a challenged motion that continually calms your many assets as you journeyed to the top floors of your field and instrument seeking elevated articulation that quietly separated you from the missing moments that we all need for full life and significant architecture. I have watched you as a father, friend, mentor always open eared to your many trails of a long and lonely step-after-step to this new love who is measured melody and years ahead of the fears of others and your unique voice that opened caves that had razors for locks. This god-man is an answer and an obligation announcing in his own name a bond denoting yes. Arriving ready to define new life with this woman of uncommon lineage, journeys, mind detection, moon chanting artist who has captured the feet, hands, heart and head of this climatic man. She will be the comma in your declarations; do not take her smile for granted. She has tasted bitter roots. You bring directive, summer fruits, sweet teas and solemn lyrics to her and her daughter's musical manuscripts.

for Nicole Margaret Mitchell and Calvin Bernard Gantt
on their day of union, July 10, 2011

PARTING LOVERS, A CLOSING WITH RENEWING POSSIBILITIES

Part One

There is more in the missing and the giving than in the
receiving. When love leaves, melody leaves, songs cease,
laughter becomes measured and brightens one's face less often.
Touch or being touched becomes highly discriminatory.
Certain touches are avoided. When love leaves,
a tearing takes place; it's like the center of one's heart being
ripped apart and exposed unfiltered
to sand or acid, like pollution. Sleeplessness
follows, one's inability to eat, and the sudden loss of weight is
inevitable for many. Others put on weight. The gaining
impacts the body: "junk food" and guilt
take the place of internal cleansing. When love is missing or
detained, there is a constant hit in the pit of the stomach,
simulating an indefinable emptiness. The loss of love is
losing of a precious part, like being lost in action,
the mission other in you. For serious lovers,
for contemplative lovers, for lovers who understand the
silklike concentration of energy and spirit required, it will take
the noise and force of hurricanes, the lava of volcanoes, and
the disconnectedness of earthquakes to confirm the undoings
of this loveship. The quieting of this kind of love is not an
often occurrence, once in a generation, maybe twice in a
lifetime. Such love is heart-rooted, sexually measured (hot),
thoughtfully shared, consistent, a slow and deliberate love
which will take the cultures and breathless thoughts of loving
others to demand its transition

Part Two

Where end to end becomes beginning to beginning.
The releasing of mind, soul, and spirit. The best cure for
transitional love is to leave lovingly. To refocus and communicate,
digest and internalize the crackings and earth-movings in
your hearts. The ultimate healers for parting lovers is rest, is
meditation, is re-evaluation of one's loveship. Healing requires
waiting time, demands thinking time, needs liberating and
insightful music. Healing is a sharing of pain with a trusted
friend talking it out. More waiting time. Avoiding blame.
Reconstructing of beautiful memories. Rebuilding thoughts.
Conversations with one's self. Meditation. Deep study and
creative productions. Exercise. Fasting. Cleansing. Cultural
inner attainment. Surrounding one's self with nature and
music, art, literature, dance; the quiet beat and rhythms of new
life. Searching softly for the simple rejuvenative powers of
nature. Reach for colors that are reflective. Search actively for
certainly, smiles, and learned exactness of blooming new love.
Take your time in the searching. Rising in this vast world are
renewal possibilities. Spring, at planting time new heat
coming. Soon.

Part Three

If parting is necessary
part as lovers.
Part as two people
who can still
smile & talk & share
the good & important
with each other.
Part
wishing each other
happy
happy life
in a world

fighting against the
men and the women,
sisters and brothers
Black as
we.

YES:
BLACK
WOMEN

YES

for those that want:
every woman a man
every man a woman,
every person an education and willing work, unexpected love
for all people
family, food, clothing, shelter, love,
frequent smiles and children swimming in glorious happiness.

For every elder a home, blooming health, few worries,
good teeth and fun-filled thank yous.
For all people,
liberating culture,
the full love of laughing children who
have been bathed in the caring eyes of
family, friends, nation.

For all people,
the inner glow that radiates peace and wisdom,
the confirming smiles of knowledge known,
the confident walk of music heard,
the quiet presence of having accepted and created beauty.

For African people
an unspoken understanding that
this is the center we gave the world

this is civilization.

BLACK WOMEN HAVE BEEN OUR ANSWERS,
NO MATTER THE QUESTIONS

the women are colors of earth and ocean
earth as life,
the beginning waters
magnificent energy.
As the women go, so go the people
determining missions
determining possibilities.
Stopping the women stops the future.

Without great teaching,
without important thoughts,
without significant deeds,
the ordinary emerges as accepted example.
Gluing the women to kitchens,
afternoon soaps,
and limiting the imagination of sightless men.
Producing a people that move with the
quickness of decapitated bodies
while
calling such movement
divine.

Possibilities: listen to the mind of women, the voices of big mama, zora neale,
sister nora, fanny lou, pretty renee, gwen brooks, queen nzinga, and warrior
mothers. All birth and prophecy, Black and heart warm, bare and precise, the
women detailing the coming collapse or rise. The best and best of youth
emerging. Telling triumphantly. If we listen, if we feel and prepare.

for Andrea Taylor and Diane D. Turner

WHY SHANI?

Old folks say that the most
courageous and committed people
are tested incessantly,
given the most intricate mountain to forge,
the deepest forest fires to quiet,
the harsher hellholes to navigate.
this journey does not inspire struggle
just unlimited offers of another path
to reconsider opposing injustice,
to stop working for the children of strangers,
to cease cleaning the wounds of the battered,
to abandon poetry.

to rise from unanswerable pain
requires a history beyond the acquisition of things,
demands work on the other side of self and self.
you have labored and researched the catalogs of the world
& refused to be separated from the poor and poorer.

your love for us is uncorrupted and contagious,
grounded in your arts, activism and the familial.
we reciprocate.

for the Baraka Family

LOVE GETS TOO MUCH CREDIT UNTIL IT FINDS YOU

you don't find love it finds you
not that love is hidden or unavailable
it's on its own mission searching for receptive souls.
love cannot be bought, sold or ordered with dinner,
cannot be charged on gold cards or revolving accounts,
cannot be bartered with food stamps, coupons or promises,
cannot be redeemed with cashier's checks or money orders.
love is seasoned and concealed in fine fire,
delicate music and accessible secrets that are quilted
to the tone of distinctive voices wrapped in un-conditions and
clear commitments
created for unique lovers who have matured
and are prepared to receive the most precious of stones
allowing love to tango its cultured language generously
and unencumbered into the essence of those
who are blessed and able to dance to the breath of the other.

ALONE MUCH OF THE TIME

The women he experienced and enjoyed life with
were fine, intelligent, children loving & smiled naturally.
Most were intuitive, self-starters & understood balance.
He avoided women with multicolored finger nails,
all the answers,
processed or finger waved hair styles,
smokers, drinkers, excessive talkers,
soap opera & talk show enthusiasts while
side-stepping women who wore clothes
glued to their bodies like balloons to air.
He didn't care for gossipers, nonreaders, big
eaters or women who were cultureless
and believed that the only use for money was to spend it.

LAINI

nurtured like her mother
wondrous,
contemplative & self absorbed.
she assigned herself a capacious journey.
new york city is a frightening certainty.
i cried when she returned
whole & enlarged & well.
still avoiding vegetables & housework.

FOR MARIAMA
SPELMAN COMMENCEMENT

The sun has blessed you.
this ritual of light,
this necessary coming out,
this gathering of sisters, mothers, grandmothers,
this awakening,
this journey,
this deciding step,
this quality walk,
this gathering of family, extended family, people,
this welcoming rootedness,
this earth warming call,
this Black high jump,
this continuation of Leslie, Alfre, Alice, and Johnnetta,*
this double-dutch of ready-women,
this calm before the yes,
this Africa across the seas,
you are our deep calculation,
embrace your numbers
come to this moment,
run to the new century without apology or slowness,
you are affirmation and clean-sound
mind your wealth internally and
never forget your name.

for Leslie Richards, Alfre Woodard, Alice Walker and Johnnetta B. Cole

MARIAMA AND BIRTH

this is the eternal truth,
        the holy truth.
there is the sun,
Africa is its first home,
millions of people of the first home are
scattered on all continents
mostly gathering wood, cleaning sewers and
misspelling liberation, freedom and art.
seeking
the answers to all the white ways, stormy skies,
ugly ways, killer ways, corrupt ways that
erase memories and life's songs of
forced migrations, cultural knowledge and planting histories
that demanded us to walk on dried bones
as if normal, right, necessary and expected of an African people,
Black people without extended families and homes.
seeking
the blue/black of our mother's enlightened tongues
and father's clarity and commitment rooted in the
defining love of books, music, dance and the
visual arts that makes us whole, human, and
divine lifemakers who understand that birth,
wanted birth, needed birth are the first rites, creative rites that complete the
circle, as
the critical openings to seasons of compressed love and learning.
seeking
the language of green & green, yes & core meanings.
seeking clear touch, initial moments, rooted in fields of flowers
tapestry: fruit, pears, apples, watermelons, grains
vegetables and final consensus to tomorrow's tomorrows,
today.
Stating emphatically the eternal truth
                        the holy truth

Birth.

for Leslie Richardson on the birth of her granddaughter,
Aminata Sun McLaurin Richards, March 16, 2017. March 16, 2017

110

OUR DAUGHTER ON LOAN

you were not to be ours forever,
yours was a short map.
some say a liberian circle
there is little human logic to your pilgrimage.
we must not deem it incomplete,
we do confirm that it was brief.

the day the sun bloodied,
the moon disappeared,
interrupting great promise and progress,
magnificent expectations.
visual artists painted muted yellows,
poets and musicians were silent and
fiction writers and dancers joined hands and tears
the second your breath stopped.

your history was still in discovery
as grandmothers, big mamas and babas declared,
"you were on loan to us,"
not a borrowed book or pawn shop watch.
your visit among us is still mystery and melody.
"tweety" birds with rhythm in their eyes.

your mother is a southern river,
your father a strong stone with baggage,
your family is Black stories, deep crops,
gathering winds, Black hurricanes in waiting.
you were washed in love and possibilities,
sun bathed in smile, tunes and cultural signatures.
why you leave us so soon?

for Kevani Zelpah Moyo, (1982-1999)

LAYLA ANAYA

arriving as the first madhubuti/hutchinson of the new millennium, she
dropped in not as fragile or delicate breast-feeder, not as blank slate, having
swam in her brilliant mother's body for three months short of a tumultuous
year, with her brain wired into the trusted mind and hearts of parents ready
for nothing less than breathing stone, brick, black earth washed in sea, ocean
& the great lakes locked into a deeper meaning than the seven pounds,
eight ounces, twenty and three-fourth inches long that she packaged,
she has parted a cloud over the earth issuing in sun, stars, and an answer
to why. she emerged with a full haired head, with eyes—black and wide—that
defined the urgency that she expected life. her fortune is that she has family,
biological and cultural, who embraced her birth like water to an out of control
forest fire in a time of world drought. she is our moment, our romare bearden
and elizabeth catlett signature, our gwendolyn brooks and dudley randall
off rhyme, our nina simore and duke ellington high swing. a gentle soul
ready to rage, ready to love, who came in the morning time to awaken
the day for those unable to sleep.

on the birth of Layla Anaya Madhubuti Lee, November 10, 2010

GABBY: All Around Gold

at fourteen she left known love
for another love of flying, pole-walking
and dancing on white floors.
not just a leap from virginia beach to des moines
it was climate change and evolution,
tidal waves, volcanoes and prayers
to embrace an extended family of
iowans and a coach from china.
this took heart, soul, silent music and strength
as she conquered a sport
not taught on the playgrounds & gyms of
natural headed black people: she exploded a dagger
into the doubts of experienced coordinators and
self-hating negroes who questioned her
"confidence and focus" and the naturalness of her hair.
she, in rejecting self-hatred, self-doubt & can't do-ness
flew as a champion into the world's living rooms
confirming talent, smiles & hair that
captured a first, gold, a sport & our hearts.

for Gabby Douglas and her all-around wins in the
Olympic gymnastics competition of 2012

BIRTH IN A TIME OF HOSTILITIES

if Black babies were loved as much as fast food,
cars, rap & hip hop, long lies and cheap
clothes made in china, indonesia and new york sweat shops
maybe, just maybe
corporate for-profit prisons, fake hair from india,
two hundred dollar sport shoes, ignorant people
claiming credit for ignorance would not be commonplace.
maybe, just maybe
accelerated smiles with high fives,
incisive conversations around the latest
discovered books, and copious yeses to green foods,
corrective weather with learned debates over the universities best suited
for children and grandchildren would dominate our discourse.

we are here to stop suffering,
to share vegetables and wheatgrass,
to confirm birth into gleeful families
we are here to tell backstories of foreparents and dark earth,
to welcome this addition to the Black circle of circles,
within an ecology of meditative silence and smiles
his name is embraced, written, notated in the holy books
and spoken in original breath:
Stokely Jamal Madhubuti Lee
we commemorate and accept this recent arrival with a word of wisdom
        ashe ashe ashe

on the birth of Stokely Jamal Madhubuti Lee, 8/26/18

THE GWENDOLYN BROOKS WRITERS CONFERENCE AT
CHICAGO STATE UNIVERSITY (C.S.U.)
From left to right: 1. Nikki Giovanni, 2. August Wilson, 3. Mari Evans, 4.
5. Lerone Bennet, Jr., 6. Elnora Daniels, 7. Gwendolyn Brooks, 8. Haki R.
Madhubuti, 9. Abrusa Ford, 10. John A. Williams, 11. Lucille Clifton

Writers' Conference - C.S.U.
For 20 years, the *Gwendolyn Brooks Center for Creative Writing and Black
Literature* sponsored an annual *Gwendolyn Brooks Writers Conference* at Chicago
State University. The major Black writers attended and were inducted into the
"Literary Hall of Fame for Writers of African Descent".

MAJOR FACTS OF LIFE

1.
we all
do
what we've
been
taught to do

2.
I
seek
the
integration of
Negroes
with
Black people.

3.
somebody
made a
mistake
(they said)
&
sent the
peace corps to
europe.

4.
went to cash
my
2020 tax refund
&
the check bounced,
insufficient funds.

POET: What Ever Happened To Luther?

he was strange weather, this luther, he read books, mainly poetry and some-
times long books about people in foreign places, for a young man he was too
serious, he never did smile, and the family still don't know if he had good
teeth. he liked music too, even tried to play the trumpet until he heard the
young miles davis. he then said that he'd try writing. the family didn't believe
him because there ain't never been no writers in this family, and everybody
knows that whatever you end up doing, it's gotta be in your blood. it's like
loving women: it's in the blood, arteries and brains. this family don't even
write letters, they call everybody. that's why the phone is off 6 months out of
a year. then again, his brother willie t. used to write long, long letters from
prison about the books he was reading by malcolm x, frantz fanon, george
jackson, richard wright and others. luther, unlike his brother, didn't smoke or
drink and he'd always be doing odd jobs to get money. even his closest
friends clyde and t. bone didn't fully understand him. while they be partying
all weekend, luther would be traveling. he would take his little money with a
bag full of food, mainly fruit, and a change of underwear and get on the
greyhound bus and go. he said he be visiting cities. yet, the real funny thing
about luther was his ideas. he was always talking about africa and black
people. he was into that black stuff and he was as light skinned as a piece of
golden corn on the cob. he'd be calling himself black and african and
upsetting everybody, especially white people. they be calling him crazy but
not to his face. anyway the family, mainly the educated side, just left him
alone. they would just be polite to him, and every child of god knows that
when family members act polite, that means that they don't want to be
around you. it didn't matter much because after his mother died he left the
city and went into the army. the last time we heard from him was in 1963. he
got put out the army for rioting. he disappeared somewhere between
mississippi and chicago. a third cousin, whose family was also polite too,
appeared one day and said that luther had grown a beard, changed his name
and stopped eating meat. she said that he had been to africa and now lived in
chicago doing what he wanted to do, writing books, she also said that he
smiles a lot and kinda got good teeth.

HEART WORK

Art has its own answers and name,
has beauty, insight and great questions too.
the poem is the unheard inquiry,
a foreign language in English and off rhyme
torturously taught by P.E. teachers
to a population bred on commercials and war games,
where the loud aesthetic is the nation's weapon
limited only by the zeros on its dollar bills.
You go substratum to decipher
the secrets of poets, musicians and hand painters.
Poetry has blanketed your heart and
your heart is like that of "Lincoln West," "Strong Men," and
"Mollie Means"
running alone on *A Street in Bronzeville* and southern back
roads

for the teachers of poetry

NATIONAL BLACK WHOLISTIC SOCIETY
July 18, 1989

From the left of photo are: Chester Grundy, David Hall, Jesse Carter, Haki R. Madhubuti, John Howell, Kamau Jawara, and Jack Thomas Jr.

For 10 years, N.B.W.S. sponsored wholistic healing & wellness retreats in upstate New York. Each retreat would host major Black thinkers in all the disciplines and each were attended by over 300 Black folks.

CLAIMING LANGUAGE, CLAIMING ART V

furious

in the destructive weather of orange hurricanes, tornadoes, avalanches and white-eyed occupiers selling cheap fear to the ignorant and terror-struck non-readers or thinkers who miraculously *know-it-all* as they claim ownership of stolen peoples, lands, ideas, music, money, dance, technology and climate denial: as fires ravish much of the international commons. It is time for colors, cleansing rain, memphis blues, mississippi greens, mind molding Black jazz and measurable yeses, to learning first, quiet moments of introspection, meditation, knowledge acquisition and livable habits prior to chasing the easy, the next line giveaways and missed melodies of poets and their poems. they who made words into life teaching, sharing, dancing indigenous vernaculars laboring for gladness and diverse tomorrows on the far side. they who transmit the lingua franca of earned accomplishments that benefit babies, children, mothers and often fathers who are not lost in crude masculinity, trapped in solitary confinement of state prisons or dead minds that focus too regularly on *get-it-for-nothing* lifestyles and no nothingness. where are the creative fighters with fists, locution and mission? where are the top writers, team creators, word finders, clear tongued poets?

flowers

world over and under, whether in denmark, ghana, china and local backyards of rocks, glass, and no hope. within apartments hidden in detroit's blackbottom, chicago's and new york's projects and the forgotten red clay of alabama. all where flowers will grow with little water, sun or helping hands. body sweet sweat of workers battling climate damage and overtime without extra pay from big box stores & for-profit colleges unable to educate pregnant roaches while student debt eclipses 1.5 trillion dollars. forcing memory, Black recall, sharing, teaching, never forgetting the wonderfully engaged wordsmiths and legendary artists often soloist of Black and tan images in short and long lines that save and give lives. this is the role call:

gwendolyn brooks, robert hayden, claude mckay,
lucille clifton, amiri baraka, margaret danner,
langston hughes, mari evans, dudley randall, léopold sédar senghor,
sterling a. brown, etheridge knight, carolyn m. rodgers,
norman jordan, julia fields, larry neal, melvin b. tolson,
nina simone, keorapetse kgositsile, oscar brown jr.
and all missing poetic Black voices who often left us
without notice, notation or preachers calling their names.

all resounding, creative and turbulent voices of Black soup,
rice milk with opened minds to consumption of raw
vegetables aided by the detox salons, from diverse poets who can read
in their sleep to awaken fresh to spot falsehood before early light. they
all come home. Presence. warrior poets, the most liberated artists in the
world navigating the language of touch, love and cayenne to the body.
wellness. they, the brilliant penetrators of bogus thought now supply us
with peaches, mangoes, pure water, yellow skinned watermelons and
critical sun screaming for the next generation of poets.
.

for Joanne Gabbin and Furious Flower, 6/19

COMPLICATED
MELODIES

WHY SHE LOVES HIM

she seldom would admit to him the reasons she was
attracted his way (not necessarily in this order):
looks, hair, tone of voice, content of his conversation, body
scent, his infectious smile,
manners, kindness & ideas. The drape of his clothes,
the quietness of his intentions & interior, care for
others, the questions he asked,
his understanding of multiple realities, his culture &
politics, his insistence upon paying for dinner,
movies & music while dating.
he is unpredictable, well-traveled with a large
mind & is unpretentious. The way he smiles
at children & gravitates toward them,
his advocacy of extended family, love of exercise,
walking, love of land.
he doesn't smoke, drink, do drugs or sleep around,
does not think it right, necessary or safe to have sex
on the first, second, third or fourth dates,
he feels that birth control is his responsibility too, clean, loves
to visit bookstores, libraries, farms,
museums and art galleries, read books,
quarterlies and magazines that have more text than
pictures, adores visual art, music, movies and theater.
respectful of women's dreams and vision,
he doesn't eat meat, fish, chicken or dairy products.
productive and economically independent,
not jealous, mentally and physically sound,
an intense caring lover and yoga practitioner. The
spiritualness of his utterances and
his presence quiets her.
the way he communicates without words is precious, and
she knows the exact location of his heart.

RISK EVERYTHING

I
at thirty-six you had tasted and tested life.
it had not conformed or confused you.
you could count your losses and loves on either hand,
a slow count. one love for each decade minus the first. in your
twenties you were blessed with a son with a man who had
detoured to a corner of your heart
without experiencing sun, healing
water or the voices of enlightened ancestors.
you traveled south and birthed a boy genius. this is to say you
always total your journey, could read a map at night and were
never without cab fare, your mother taught you her pain and
laughter, your
grandmother said, "men needed excuses." your father proved
her correct. your aunts schooled you in the lies of women. it
was left to you to
locate the intimate and intricate truths. your best girl
friend taught you how to fix
cars that you drove as if your soul was glued to the steering
wheel of better destinations.

you found that men were like unchartered continents
most are undeveloped nations,
often tribal in their limitations,
too many unable to reach their own knowledges
or questions. having your own son to raise,
you refuse to suffer for boys in grown folks clothes.
in your fourth decade you allowed a man into your life who was
not looking for you.
he spoke in poems and strange food.
he looked at you for a full year before he said yes.
he realized that you were a compass, a liberated zone, careful
and sure, discriminating. lean with love.

II
you take my ebony stone and I take yours.
breathe on it, touch it to your heart. Like stones we
are not new to earth or love, we've planted seeds at
    midnight.
we approach the sun cleansed. whole. awaken to
    shape a memory.
no longer young our expectations are like the
    stones:
hard melody, created in sweet heat.
    everlasting. focused.
shaped in deep histories by the unimpressionable
medications of struggle and deep-rooted greens.
we are the fundamental witness to each other's
requirements, supportive and thankful.
these stones are not to be cast away. ever.
they carry spirited devotion and tender joy
they are our markings and maps,
they are our delicate signatures.

TEE ONE IN A COMPLEX WORLD

this woman
does good when good is unnoticeable or advertised,
she carries rocks to the dams of beavers,
writes memorandum of possibilities for single mothers,
vows publicly for the security of children,
hears the prophets' voices from the roots of oak trees,
would give you her leg
if she didn't have to walk.

this woman
can read a smile in evil,
studies the earth's waterfalls,
understands iambic pentameter,
reads the sacred texts of Africa and Israel,
she sings the lyrics of Shirley Horn
while monitoring the intricate speech of her progeny
who converses in coded alphabet and colors.

her kisses are climactic
an oral lover who has a fondness for carrot juice.
she memorizes the sensitive nerves of her men and
attends to the feet of the difficult musician on her block.
her decisive word to him was no
as she prepared to travel foreign waters
to kiss new trees.

this woman is artful earth opening for the seeds awaiting her.

RECESSION PROOF SEX

the unheard screams
in the missing uneasy lives of the
unprotected innocents imported from china, europe,
russia, africa, india, the americas and cracks in between,
ever growing numbers of not yet teenagers,
clean girls, smiling sisters and daughters with inadequate fathers and
    brothers,
crippled mothers, families and hollow governments to nurture their
    tomorrows.
they fuel the oldest recession proof profession in the world;
claiming the young and youngest with failed promises and
quick lies spoken, written, read and rewritten by men
in the service of men as history denies the victims their own
stories, memories or horror voices guaranteeing that
misogyny remains the language of commerce
that keeps the enslaved ignorant, beautiful, drugged and submissive.
sold and traded on an under/over ground world market
to men demanding profit, pleasure and "immortality"
by way of the vaginas of virgins.
the muted cries, the waterfall screams disappear
under the weight and rape of youth being stolen, defiled and brain damaged.

most innocents do not have sex as an act of love or pleasure;
they sex to procreate,
they sex to survive,
they sex to eat,
they sex to protect their children,
they sex to pay their father's and husband's debts,
they sex to better their lives,
they sex for pennies or less,
they sex to join families and tribes together,
they sex as expression of love expecting love,
they sex as an act of work,
they sex to maintain families,
they sex to keep men,
they sex to satisfy the lust of men,

they sex to question and answer,
they sex for education, promotion, and for others,
they sex for passports, green cards and visas
they sex for protection,
they sex as an act of religious obligation in the service
        of the pathological patriarch.
girls becoming women learn liberation on the streets of brutality
snatching knowledge, information, running routes and
modern underground railroads from the mouths of
customers, johns, tricks, coworkers, new friends and husbands.
most seeking good dreams, love and personal selection
quietly and systematically many plan to steal away into the night to
painfully make a life as goes the songs of billie holiday
somewhere, one day, finding my own way.

for Maxine Graves Lee

MATURITY

emma jean aged one night
back in september of '63
it was after them girls
had received death in alabama
on their knees
praying
to the same god,
in the same church,
in the same space,
she prayed.

she aged that night
after the day had gone
and left her with her thoughts.
left her with the
history of her people in
america.
emma jean matured that night
and knew that in a country
that killed the children
under
the eyes of *their* god   that
she nor her people
were safe.

emma jean
decided back in september of '63
that she would let her people
know that they were not safe in
america
this is what she has done
and is doing   if she has not found you
look for her   kiss & hug her
thank her and then help her
to help us
mature.

for Judy Richardson and Diane Nash

131

BLACKGIRL LEARNING

she couldn't quote french poetry
that doesn't mean that she ain't read any
probably not
tho gwendolyn brooks & margaret walker
lined her dresser.

she did tell me that
the bible was pure literature
& she showed me her own poetry.
far beyond love verse (& it didn't rhyme)
she wrote about her man.

she said that her man
worshiped her,
he wasn't there.
she told me that he had other things to do:

learning to walk straight.

THE PETTY SHELL GAME

with raped memories and clenched fists, with small
thoughts and needless time we indulge in destruction
bathing ourselves in comedy and fraudulent posture:
willa mae is going with big daddy t and iula is
   pregnant and don't know who the father is,
   cleavon said that the father is "we the people."

quite a profound statement among losers and people
beaten into the gutter and like desperate rats continue
to destroy with:
   richard g. is a "faggot" and pretty johnny is bald
   under that rag on his head, rev. jones is going
   with sister mary & sister emma & sister sara
   &   but
the important issue here always, especially among the
   young is
where is the party this weekend &
where you get that boss smoke, man?
yet, as the hipped shipped often say, "only fools
work" not daring to take into consideration that
"fools" built the western world and raped the rest of it.
yes, "only fools work" as we non-fools every early
monday morn fight each other for position outside
the state welfare department.

SOME OF THE WOMEN ARE BRAVE

her strength may have come from
not having good things early in life
like
her own bed, unused clothes,
"good looks" and uncritical friends
she also missed musical insights
from the knee of her great grandmother's wisdom.
whatever path she took
she was learning to become small danger.

organizer of mothers,
overseer of broken contracts,
a doer of large deeds,
unafraid of sky scrapers & monotone
bureaucrats.
monotones labeled her demands crippling & unusual.
she urged drinkable water, working elevators,
clean playgrounds, heat, garbage collection
and the consolation of tenants dreams.

many damned her,
others thought her professional agitator & provocateur
dismissing her as a
man hating bulldagger
that was communist inspired.

she was quick burn against the enemy
a stand up boxer unattached to niceties
and the place of women.
she was waterfalls in the brain
her potency as it comes
needs to be packaged & overnight expressed
to Black homes; to be
served with morning meals.

for the Women of SNCC

WINTERMAN

janice was winter
she had been made cold by
years of maltreatment rough years
of loneliness and false companionship
and now in the middle of her time
she refused to ever take another chance with a
blackman.

janice cursed the race. didn't see no good that black
people ever done. raised on a plantation where her
father was a sharecropper
she watched her mother, in her twilight years, steal away to jesus. the bible
was more than solution, more than heaven after earth, it was food and water.
it was ideas and values steeped in fear and peaceful salvation.

janice ran north at twenty and between her twenty-first and twenty-seventh
year visited every store front church on the west and south sides of chicago.
she now fashions herself a true missionary of the living gospel. her mission
was to save black men from their evil ways. she wanted black men to be like mr.
golding, the husband of the white woman she did day work for. mr. golding
took care of his family, had a big house and ate dinner with his family every
night that he didn't have to work late (he worked late at least twice-a-week).

most black men thought janice was fine but foolish. after loving her many
would brakelight fast. disappear, most leaving without an explanation. it
came out later that some of them didn't like being preached to at the point
of sexual climax. others felt that she prayed too much and were
uncomfortable with being compared to judas. after as many men as churches,
janice in her thirty-fifth year decided to close her legs and like her mother
give her life, completely and unshared, to the only man in her life she
declared had never failed her. jesus would now be the only man in her heart.
it is not known exactly when during that year she was called but rumor has it
that the *ultimate light* touched her the day after billy william, her last lover,
started seeing her best and only friend minnie lou turner.

janice cursed the race, didn't see no good in black people. She turned slavishly
and slowly toward her employers and began to live in, arlington heights,
illinois which was clean, peaceful and few black people lived there.
it was winter and windy
it was cold and white   and
jesus,
sweet, sweet jesus
was her man.

STRUGGLE

some called her
sunshine others berryblack
she was woman twice
laid way way back
her smile was winning-wide
her teeth glowed and captured light
she was woman twice
Men thought her mighty nice

Deep black off brown and Mississippi grown Lula Mae was careful. she had
experienced the heartaches, heard the stories and often hid the tears. Lula
Mae was more watcher and listener now. Yes, her emotions were still there,
real & womanly strong but they had failed her too often in the past. her
lovers had left memories that distorted her forehead and scars that even she
didn't want to acknowledge.

(pretty willie g left his fist print under her left ear, larry the pimp provided
her with a dislocated hip and baby frank left her $3000 in debt with
promises of short life if she mentioned his whereabouts.)

Lula mae now sought other signs of caring. She wanted relationships that
were
not so one-sided, short-termed or physically risky, she looked for verbal
confirmation, evening phone calls, unexpected love notes and deep back and
foot massages at the day's end. Lula mae, not yet 30, knew that she was
special,
knew that her capacity for love was unusual and also knew that the next man
in her life would understand and appreciate this specialness before he got
any of it.

what will it be?
when will Blackmen learn that
fist & feet against the teeth
is like removing the heart of a people.
who will teach us that slaps & kicks & verbal lashings
detour sharing, stop bonding,

destroy unifiers, retard respect & eliminate
connecting vision.
what will it be?
what messenger, what unmuted voice
will clarify touching

detail body contact without blackeyes?
what caller will articulate
disagreements without boxing,
love
without force.
where are the bold & rejuvenated men
and women that will head this most needed of
revolutionary struggles?

BIG MOMMA

finally retired   pensionless
from cleaning somebody else's house
she remained home to clean
the one she didn't own.

in her kitchen where we often talked
the *chicago tribune* served as a tablecloth
for the two cups of tomato soup that went
along with my weekly visit & talkingto.

she was in a seriously-funny mood
& from the get-go she was down, realdown:

>   roaches around here are like
>   letter on a newspaper
>   or
>   u gonta be a writer, hunh
>   when u gone write me some written
>   or
>   the way niggers act around here
>   if talk cd kill we'd all be dead.

she's somewhat confused about all this blackness
but said that it's good when negroes start putting themselves
first and added: we've always shopped at the colored stores,
& the way niggers cut each other up round
here every weekend that whiteman don't
haveta
worry bout no revolution specially when he's
gonta haveta pay for it too, anyhow all he's
gotta do is drop a truck load of dope out
there on 43rd st. & all the niggers & yr
revolutionaries
be too busy getten high & then they'll turn
round
and fight each other over who got the mostest.

we finished our soup and I moved to excuse myself,
as we walked to the front door she made a last comment:
>   now *luther* I knows you done changed a lots but if
>   you can think back, we never did eat too much pork
>   round here anyways, it was bad for the belly.
I shared her smile and agreed.
touching the snow lightly I headed for 43rd st.
at the corner I saw a brother crying   while
trying to hold up a lamp post,
thru his watery eyes I cd see big mama's words.

at sixty-eight
she moves freely, is often right
and when there is food
eats   joyously with her own
real teeth.

for all Big Mamas, Grandmamas and Nanas

FUTURE

first
it is between the Black and the Black
come
not as empty earth,
not as wasted energy,
not as apologetic color consciousness,
not as fools blinded to light,
not as imitation cardboard.

come
as gifted lovers
eyes bright & daring life,
come
as ripening fruit
quick smiles and joyous words.
come
woman to man
man to woman
pursuing the way of life
within the colors of vision
between the
Black and the Black.

BLACKWOMAN

blackwoman.
will define herself, naturally, will
talk/walk/live/& love her images, her
beauty will be. The only way to be is
to be blackman take her. U don't need
music to move; yr/movement toward her
is music. & she'll do more than dance.

1968

WOMEN WITH MEANING

she is small and round,
round face and shoulders connected to half-sun breast,
on a rounded stomach that sits on rounded buttocks,
held up by short curved legs and circular feet,
her smile reveals bright teeth and when it comes,
her eyes sing joy and her face issues in gladness,
she is brilliant beauty.
she likes colors,

her hair, which is worn in its natural form, is
often accented with vivid, cheerful scarfs. her make-up
is difficult to detect, it compliments her oak-colored skin,
suggesting statuesque music. her scent is fresh mango
and morrocan musk. her clothes are like haitian paintings,
highly noticeable during her rhythmic walks,
as she steps like a dancer.

she is a serious woman,
her values,
her ideas,
her attitudes,
her actions are those of a reflective mind.
her child is her life,
her people her future,
she and her child live alone and the brothers
speak good words about them.

the brothers,
married and unmarried, want to help her.
it is difficult to be with her and not
lose one's sense of balance,
one's sense of place and wisdom.
that is what caring does.
her aloneness
hurts and tears at the inside of serious men.
some of the older men have tried

to tie her heart into theirs but
the commitment was never enough.
her sense of honor and history,
her knowing of sisterhood and rightness
force her to sleep alone each night.

the brothers continue to speak good words about her,
many
when thinking of
her smile.
others light candles and pray.
some send her notes, gifts and poems,
all
hoping for the unexpected.

WONDERMENT

LEAVING LARGE VOICES

RAPE: THE MALE CRIME

there are mobs & strangers
in us
who scream of the women
wanted and
will get
as if the women
are ours for the
taking.

our mothers, sisters, wives and
daughters ceased to be the
women men want   we think of them as
loving family   music & soul   bright wonderments.
they are not locker room talk
not the hunted lust or   dirty
cunt burnin hoes.
bright wonderments are excluded   by association as
blood & heart   bone & memory
& we will destroy a rapist's knee caps,
& write early grave on his thoughts
to protect them.

it will do us large to recall
when the animal in us rises
that all women are someone's
mother, sister, wife or daughter
and are not fruit to be stolen when hungry.

Rape is not a reward for warriors
it is war itself
a deep, deep tearing, a dislocating of
the core of the womanself.
rape rips heartlessly
soul from spirit,
obliterating colors from beauty and body
replacing melody and music with

rat venom noise and uninterrupted intrusion and beatings.

a significant few of their
fathers, brothers, husbands, sons
and growing strangers
are willing to unleash harm on the earth
and spill blood in the eyes
of
maggots in running shoes
who do not know the sounds of birth
or respect the privacy of the human form.
No!
Means No!
even when men think
that they are "god's gift to women"
even after dropping a week's check & more
on dinner by the ocean,
the four tops, temptations and intruders memory tour,
imported wine & rose that captured her smile,
suggested to you private music & low lights
drowning out her unarticulated doubts.

Question the thousand years teachings
crawling through your lower depths and
don't let your little head
out think your big head.
No! means No!
even when her signals suggest yes.

*Madhubuti has been doing liberation work for men and boys for over
fifty years. For additional information on becoming an anti-rapist
see the essay, "Rape: The Male Crime" in the addendum.*

ABORTION

she,
walla (queen) anderson
miss booker t. washington jr. high of 1957,
miss Chicago bar maid of 1961
had her first abortion at 32
after giving birth to
john (pee wee) Jackson at 14,
mary smith at 15 and a half,
janice wilson at 17,
dion jones at 19,
sara jones at 21,
and
richard (cream) johnson at 27.

on a sun-filled day
during her 32nd year
after
as many years of aborting
weak men who would not stand
behind their own creations
she
walla (queen) anderson
by herself alone without consultation
went under the western butchers
to get her insides
out.

IS TRUTH LIBERATING?

if it is truth that binds
why are there
so many lies   between
lovers?

if truth is liberating
why
are people told:
they look good when they don't
they are loved when they aren't
everything is fine when it ain't
glad you're back when they're not.

Black people in america
may not be made for the truth
we wrap our lives in disco and
Sunday morning sermons
while
selling false dreams to our children.

lies
are refundable,
can be bought on our revolving
charge cards   as
as we all catch truth
on the next go round
if
it doesn't hurt

for Beverly Guy-Sheftall, Alice Walker and bell hooks.

MAYA: We Honor Our Own

your voice bridged genre,
in concert with Malcolm, Killens, Baldwin and Brooks
it matured us,
stamped us to ourselves,
impelled a recognition that had been contradicted
by priest and anthropologist,
by banker and architect.
your voice, able, harmonious and emphatic,
willfully free and angular
dared to confront our fears,
invade our interiors and weak utterances.
Maya, a wandering call back,
our precise reminder.
no longer a test pilot,
welcome
poet who can boogie-down.
you are among the last of the great trees,
high questioner, master wordgiver and witness.
you've paid our dues,
there is no copy, clown or apology here.
we find home in your presence.

for Maya Angelou, Howard University
Heart's Day 2004

IN OUR TRADITION

his woman is sitting on the back porch,
insects feed off the sweat of her lean body,
they have just finished making love.
she hurried out of the room

to cry away from his smiles & smell.
after the flood of '95
she had promised herself that before
she loved him again
she would take to the fields, break bread with nuns
look wolves in the eye & kneel before the sea of light
to armor her heart away from his touch.

her breath young & spirited,
her eyes lucent & unequivocal
betrayed the armor about her heart

it is he who promised her heartlove
it is she who questions the love in
his heart.

for the brothers

MY BROTHERS

my brothers i will not tell you
who to love or not love
i will only say to you
that
Black women have not been
loved
enough.

i will say to you
that
we are at war & that
Black men in america are
being removed from the
earth
like loose sand in a windstorm
and that the women Black are
three to each of us.

no
my brothers i will not tell you
who to love or not love
but
i will make you aware of our
self-hating and hurting ways.
make you aware of whose bellies
you dropped from.
i will glue your ears to those images
you reflect who are not being
loved.

THE DAMAGE WE DO

he loved his women
weak & small
so that he would not tire
of
beating them.
he sought the weakest & the smallest
so that they couldn't challenge
his rage of boxing
their heads up against refrigerators,
slamming their hands in doors,
stepping on them like roaches,
kicking them in their centers of life.
all of his women
were
weak and small and sick
& he an
embarrassment to the human form
was not an exception in america.

VIOLENCE AGAINST WOMEN

violence against women in a violent nation(s),
violence against women in a football nation(s),
violence against women in an offensive war nation,
          where patriarchy is manliness and the bible is law
          in the name of god, nation and man as head of home, workplace and
earth.
violence against women in a basketball nation,
violence against women in a 24/7 war on women nation where authorities
          give a wink, smile and nod to domestic and anti-abortion violence
          where 90 percent of
          police and military are men and rape kits go untested and the culture
is anti-women
where combat is hand to head in the home and on the battlefield
violence against women in a baseball nation,
violence against women in a male decision-making nation and world
          where war is made for insulting a president's father and oil
          where man is made in the image of god and is a man's man.
violence against women in a world where men run it without question
or opposition,
violence against women in a husband's and father's wife beating, wives
and children nation,
          where men sell women and children, trade and barter women,
violence against women in a male S & P 500 (CEO and money first nation)
violence against women where congress and the supreme court are bought
and sold in
a monied white men nation,
violence against women in its war on the LGBTQ[1] communities where lies,
fabrication,
          money and more money talks, rules and legislates.

_____

*Lesbian, Gay, Bisexual, and Transgendered communities

155

violence against women in all cultures, workplaces, bedrooms, kitchens, speech,
social media, art, psychology, television, film, radio, video, classrooms,
politics, literature, history, sports, courts, print media, fraternities, sororities,
churches, mosques, temples, synagogues, families and everywhere
violence is expected, accepted, encouraged and elevated as answer
and loudly excused solution.
violence against women with fist, knives, guns, chain saws, poison,
penises, and all acts of terror waiting to be invented and thought of by
each and future generations of men.

violence against women as in "she made me do it" or in *blame the victim*,
this is a hungry and angry
violence against women world where our greatest misgiving is our own

silence.

our own revisions.

MESSAGE TO OUR SONS

son,
do not forget the women killed
by the whites & men negro made white.
do not disregard the women Black
killed for closing their legs to
bodies foreign to their insides,
for preserving the culture of their foreparents,
for daring to be the just.
son, let your memory not erase
or betray the sacred teachings of
these   women.   mothers,   sisters,   lovers   and   wives
whom the world has transgressed against,
record their tracks in code and memory.
my sons do not neglect our women nor
forgive those who have *violated*
a precious part of you.

A POEM FOR QUINCY JONES AND TOO MANY OTHERS

it is actual and prophetic   that
when the money comes
when the fame and autograph seekers arrive,
when there is something to share & wear,
that the root is forced into basements,
backrooms becoming an aching embarrassment.

acts toward early Black lovers become frigid clichés
(after children wrecking & torturous, rise to the pinnacle)
the root is now tolerated baggage & excessive worry,
for him the current revelation is that
"people are just people"
converting the universe into one gigantic lovefest.
exempting
the berrycolored nappyheaded   rustykneed
exempting
the widehipped   biglipped   cherrybrown   yellowblack women.

his eyes have gone pink sucking
venom from the people
who less than a word ago
less than a few missed meals ago
used his ass as a shoe shiner.
    tap tap dance do the bounce now
    do the white boy Richard 357 magnum yr car
    shoot death in yr toe freebase raw brilliance
    fire up tap tap tap dance run out da pain in da
    brain   supernegro

stardom is the ultimate drug,
fame fogs tradition. dismembers values
& elevates egos to cocaine highs.
idol status
is volcanic to the insides   evaporates memory
& neutralizes kindness.
the *root   the Black root*

the unbought memory of the culture
flows red and liberated in the women.
when the women are traded and reduced to
matrilineal burning bitches
bleeding sets in   family's decay
rendering generational destruction
producing final stop orders.

ask your mama.

JUSTICE AS THE PUREST MOTIVATION

when you have conquered the hurt,
felt the missing letters in the word-sentences
to come but will not.

when you realized that you measured
your own contemplations to a master
who refused to accept credit,
when credit is due.

when did you comprehend that a scholar could
out dress a jazz musician, think beyond law & lies,
smile in a manner that disarmed cornbread
fed enemies of the bronze age and note that,
that was only the beginning?

his wisdom was wired to our ears,
speaking in whispers, his ethical flowers
split stones, favored clarity and fables,
knew that women, one named Geneva Crenshaw,
were the source of wonderment, love and telling questions.

he took failure as a challenge, as all of
his "first" became green doors for others
creating a lexicon of, "come on in" and
ready yourself for a fight, america is not finished.

no was a foreign language and
he a human climate changer encouraging
students and others to sample the multiple weathers
of his many seasons, bringing and leaving fresh air,

warmth, cultural urgency and complexity as in,
"absolutely is and absolutely not."

metaphor and direct action, poetry and prose,
he drew the line and crossed it, pushing us ever forward
never to compromise the *lingua franca* of
hope and possibilities, enlarging and legitimizing
the performance of struggle, resistance and human confirmation,

he was our justice-wing hurricane, tsunami and silence.
they never saw him coming.

for Janet, his children and us remembering Derrick Bell, (1931-2011)

THE LAST FIRST

not the first heavyweight champion of the world,
        airline pilot, quarterback in the NFL, college graduate,
        doctor, teacher, big league baseball player, preacher-pastor,
        ceo, mountain climber, university president, entrepreneur,
        heart surgeon, inventor, governor or poet.
not the first mathematician, physicist, engineer, supreme court justice,
        fastest man alive, publisher, reporter, ambassador, entertainer,
        four-star general, best-selling author, executive chef, sergeant major,
        scientist, basketball hall-of-famer, economist, secretary of state,
        noble prize winner, astronaut, law enforcer, chair of the joint chiefs,
        senator, first responder or state legislator.
not the best trumpet player alive, bank president, husband, father,
        organic farmer, rapper's rapper or coach's coach.
not an undefined question looking for an answer or
        hidden agenda claiming the authority of one.
not an exploiter of the commons.
        is the green hands nurturing fields, crops and rain forests,
        is the water, food, education, clean energy, preventive health
        and intellect required.
        is the humanitarian connecting music and economy, writing political
            notes
        legible to professionals, novices, students and elders the world over.
        is the community organizer maneuvering citizens' campaigns
        expecting to implant knowledge, consent and saneness on
            impracticability
        as renegade[1] and renaissance[2] expand the *can* in *we* and *yes*
at the early-light of this promising century
not the last, is the first
barack hussein obama, president.

for Michelle, Malia and Sasha Obama

---

[1] Secret Service code names for the President-Elect.
[2] Secret Service code names for the First Lady.

THE SECRET OF HIS SUCCESS

barack obama is the holder
of the keys to the white house
the one in washington on pennsylvania avenue
that represents the nation that his people built.
be they un-credited, relegated to back doors,
kitchens, wine cellars and after dark clean-up duty
performed in physical and mental chains carefully chanting
"yes sir, boss" with a grin and heads bowed, yet unbeater.

today, there is a Black man with
keys to the front door of the white house.
living there with a Black woman who
stopped his young, searching heart,
helped to unlock his history, heritage and religion
gave him two daughters, a brother and
a live-in mother, all darker than he is.

barack obama
birthed by a free euro-american from kansas
and a liberated african from kenya
is teaching his daughters the first lessons
that earned him the keys to the white house:
he stretched and amplified his persistent mind, traveled
found his calling, voice and his people,
designed a path, purpose and excelled in claiming other cultures
and never, I say never,
learned the acts of niggerization
or accepted victimhood.

for Michelle, Malia and Sasha Obama

MORE POWERFUL THAN GOD?

More powerful than Christianity, Islam, Judaism,
        Hinduism, Buddhism, Sikhism, Jainism and love.

More powerful than Shintuism, Ancestor Veneration,
        Evolutionism, decency, Creationism, Monotheism,
        Freedom, Atheism, Philosophy, Science and fear.

More powerful than Spirituality, Sociology, Marxism,
        Secularism, Zionism, Nationalism, Climate change,
        Democracy, Humanism, and the lives of children.

More powerful than Confucianism, morality, Communism,
        logic, Yoruba and Zulu beliefs, The Commons,
        Black Theology, Native American-First Nations People's beliefs,
        Egyptology, psychology, joy and truth.

More powerful than peace, prayers and all of the United States'
        cultural, political, financial systems,
        and reigns *as the God* of cowardly politicians,
        without a close second and *untouchable* is:

        The National Rifle Association

THE N.R.A. AND ITS SUPPORTER'S MANTRA

After most gun multiple killings
we are preached, inundated and sound bitten with
"guns don't kill people"
neither do
knives, hatches, hammers, kitchen sinks,
bricks nor logs kill people.
"people kill people"
with guns,
knives, hatchets, hammers, kitchen sinks,
bricks, logs from trees and other objects.
yet if
the teachers have a chance to find and
pick up a knife, hatchet, hammer, kitchen sink,
brick or tree log to defend children against the same
or better yet, run,
it is still all but impossible to
outrun or karate-kick
bullets.

*In memory of the twenty children and six adults killed on
December 14, 2012 in Newtown, Connecticut and the hundreds of children,
teenagers and adults who are killed each week in America.*

DENIED SUBSTANTIAL AND FUNDAMENTAL CREATION

it is now in the
who
you love that may
determine that you
die
without regard to the
human-person perfected in you as
caregiver, musician, educator, linguist, parent,
carpenter, spit and polish marine, visual artist, son, daughter,
actor, professional entertainer, m.d., student, clear-thinker,
athlete, interior designer, book editor, looking-for-work dog walker,
spiritual gift-giver seeking the beautiful side of yes
in a world of no and demonization of the "other"
by the "righteous" of all cultures.   who misreads and misinterprets the cultur-
al canonical,
spiritual text of the last millennium?
what holy text speaks lovingly or accurately to the human condition
& intelligence, global warming, internet searches,
high speed rail, space stations, the imagination of artists,
the vision of architects & mathematicians,
the biology of love within & across languages, borders & hearts?
escalating the genetics of internal bonding
with the same sex and melody as all species naturally do.
what god ordered the hammer repeatedly beating into his head
merely because he openly lived & loved the way
he was created to by his/your
God?

for David Kato, the Ugandan gay activist who was assassinated as a result
of his work and life struggles against madness in his native country

NATIVE COUNTRY IN THE PERSON OF ONE

weaponize ignorance
legitimizes the unknowing of self.
the inability to decode negatives
is the result of unchained education on
after-burners, whips and muskets.

a questioning man is as dangerous
as hot-sauce on pancakes.
it is the unknown ideas of why and the
manifest mission of the enslavers who
drive the inquiring men/women to ponder, enlist and
force open the field doors, books and secrets of
white-only water fountains, keep out fear-makers,
ghost separatists culture, wealth-hoarders and gun scientists.

what is the pedagogy of the upward poor?
to locate their authentic minds,
to impede the cycle of landlessness, hunger and unconsciousness,
to know the profound distinction between yes, yeah and yessah boss,
to realize that kindness and empathy are not weaknesses but character,
to conclude that knowledge acquisition is not global or assured,
to deduct that the loss of insects, birds, mammals and south and north poles
is evidence that we are killing our planet,
to imagine, recognize, create and construct life answers that work
to confirm that Black, Brown and People of Color cultures are answers and
not the problem.
in a life knocking the hell out of a century,
with a history of breathing the same pages as du bois, locke, wife susan and
the thinking, ownership and rulership classes of the world
you are able to still swim fishlike with local and world museums,
inventorying the deadly landscapes of european supremacy and
witness the articulation and architecture of alien rule,
denial, genocide and white ascendency as you issued
your own notice of war, reconstruction, clear language and study.

still breast-stroking at ninety-eight with Black vision, wisdom, and right steps.
indeed reverend doctor you "do us proud" and will be recorded
from jubilant congregations of all sacred-texts that you
native-country's son done good, real good and still
daily unlocking lost and discovered pages of our precious texts

Professor Edmund W. Gordon's 98th Birthday and the Ribbon Cutting
for the Edmund W. Gordon Brooklyn Laboratory Charter School
and for the memory of his dear wife, Dr. Susan Gordon.

FOR R. KELLY

If you have daughters?
how you gointa
protect them
from the somebodies just
like you?

2003

IN A TIME OF DEVASTATION AND REFLECTION

1.
and the earth cracked
breaking life,
legs, street corners, tomorrows,
prompting whys, whats, wheres, next?
necessitating recalls of history,
psychology, stolen economies, foreign armies,
the underside of traitors
dressed in europe, the new world
and the betrayed colors of self & self.

and then, the earth separated.
an updated missed message eclipsed
man-made catastrophes by the millions.
as children consume contaminated water & dirt,
as helicopters dropped paratroopers & excuses
on a nation unprepared for the emptiness of
international promises, smiles, hedge funds
and calls for self-reliance & reparations.

2.
and yes, a u.s. vetted world responded
with care, funds and tears,
with monies, controlled and paralyzed
by suspected off-shore agencies,
charities & wolves.
unaware of local stories, poems and culture,
ignorant of failed rulerships, ruled and braided hair.

what of the children?
of the clear, clean, innocent, muted voices
in the conflicted question of resettlement, reconstruction
and land ownership all following the money
on this soil of caste, class and color
whose cries will go unnoticed by
davos, capitol hill, 10 downing street, the G-20
and the descendants of napoleon bonaparte
and his defeated armies and history.

3.
haiti has returned to its creation
bricks, rocks, sand, dirt & tree-less.
who will plan their rebirth,
lead a reverse brain drain,
issue calls for poets, architects, musicians,
earthquake engineers, doctors, teachers, writers &
caretakers of the earth?
who will accurately define haiti's enemies,
those who are black & black,
white and white, multicolored
with the starting image of new thought, work, honest visions?
after haiti's national burial,
grieving and
the healing of the least of us
who will demand comfort and renewal,
enlightened governance and beauty.

hopefully, not the same old suspects in black suits.
certainly, you can call my name.

for Edwidge Danticat, Dr. Ron Daniels and the people of Haiti

ROBERT BLY: For The Years of His Poetics, Wisdom and Art

I
I also wear vests
influenced from the jazz-bop years
of very clean and clear musicians.
my vests lack the color and calling of those
accenting your generous landscape and language.
your speech is like the manhattan tunnels
delivering musical trains to islands as
diverse as brooklyn, chicago, little rock, utah,
london, oakland and the lakes of minnesota and michigan.
you write "wildness and domesticity" calm complications
claiming the wisdom of two centuries of poetry
floating full bodied in your active veins and voice,
running, running, running.

II
you, an architect and seer of
poetry of the outdoors, mountains and wild winds,
poetry that women read and sing at dawn and dusk,
poetry that free men from the traps of ugly maleness,
poetry that defines glorious possibilities that literature demands,
poetry that runs with rams, dogs, non-readers, children,
dancers, carpenters, reflexologists and blind editors,
poetry of adjectives, adventure and teachers
as in we are the tangents to your inclusive circle.
poetry of water, earth, trees, fire and cultures' tongue,
poetry as the art centered testimony
and drum that civilizations require.

III
you occupy a territory crying for
saneness, quiet and anti-fear as in
water consumed at deepest thirst in
vistas devastated by "greed is not enough"
corporatist gods who have never read
Whitman, Frost, Anna Akhmatova, Twain, Wendell Berry,

Adrienne Rich, William Carlos Williams, Rumi, Denise Levertov,
Etheridge Knight, Donald Hall, Gwendolyn Brooks, or Robert Bly.
yet, on this day of days students on all continents
carry, study and quote your poetry, prose and wisdom
often grounded and perfectly sounded in recently formed
MFA classes and on the back streets of America beyond
the sights, squeals and hunger of an angry rulership:
the one percent who recycle madness imbedded in 15 second
commercials on 500 channels that do not sleep and
never stop counting ill gotten money.

IV
i call you poet.
as an aged member of the league of poets,
i reserve that right and prerogative.
poet, first name of a vest wearer
unafraid of reaching and reading across cultures,
cities and campfires of the traditionalist and current.
traveler of the first order, translator and word anthropologist.
call you questioner of the unordinary, big breath,
woman lover, brother man and stationary wanderer,
a line maker, a singer of verse and song, a mandated story teller
connecting decades, generations and centuries,
not walking on water but feet firmly planted on earth,
red soil, the ultimate protector of the commons and correct tongue.

V
to the gathering of many and more who
state yes, and of course to unscripted, unsanctioned
and certainly uncensored knowledge of this man
who loves poetry that is also found on the side avenues,
the wrong side of the tracks, among unread books,
hanging outside the missing minds of the young innocents
who so desperately crave kind words, rhyming words,
words of discipline, love and magical meaning.
calling all able thinkers, word collectors and peace creators to
follow your charge as carefully and exactly as
free verse allows, requesting us to write well,

think and contemplate large and small,
share necessary and good work universally,
learn an instrument and second language,
search for and tell truths confirmed by children and
never forget that lies are contagious, paid for by
"citizens united" and thus multiply
like roaches in heat on a bed of sugar and are
damning, drug-drunken, deadly,
anti-poetry, pro-fear and anti-art.

in a life renouncing ignorance and folly
you have given us prospect, secrets, white hair and
a voice unable to sleep,
emerging in the morning time and at midnight
always on point to sound the alarm.

for Ruth Bly, October 19, 2012

JAMES SPADY, ELEANOR TRAYLOR,
TONI CADE BAMBARA, HAKI MADHUBUTI, SONIA SANCHEZ

REPARATIONS: The United States' Debt Owed to Black People

Debt is owed to African people for centuries of unpaid
    forced labor, suffering,
    death in the tens of millions and the systematic
    seasoning and
    victimization of an entire race of people.

Debt is owed for the willful and brutal separation of
    African people from their
    land, mothers from children, husbands from wives
    and families, children
    from fathers and mothers and a whole people
    from their African land, culture and
    consciousness that defined them, and gave them
    substance and
    memory.

Debt is owed for redefining all Africa people, women,
men and children as
slaves and sub-humans not deserving of salvation,
universal love,
kindness, human consideration, education and fair
compensation for all
forms of labor.

Debt is owed for the designation of African people as
property, three-fifth
humans whose only use is to slave from sun-up to
sun-down, for slave "owners", therefore
reduced African people to the category of animals
accorded less care than that of pigs,
sheep, cattle and dogs.

Debt is owed for the inhuman treatment of Africans
forced to slave for the sole
benefit of Europeans, Americans and others
for leftover food, clothes
and sleeping space and whose worth and value
was determined by their
production in building wealth for Europe, America
and its people.

Debt is owed for the brutal, ordered, encouraged and
unrelenting rape of
African women by white human (aka slave) traders
and "owners", thereby producing a
nation of half-black, half-white children whose
color, status, history and consciousness
branded them forever as "bastards," thereby creating
a color, class and cultural
consciousness that to this day continues to rip the
hearts out of African
people maintaining a vicious circle of self-hatred,
self-destruction and denial in them.

Debt is owed for centuries of ruthless, planned and
destructive looting and
wholesale theft of Africa's people, land and mineral
wealth for the sole
purpose of creating wealth for Europe, the United States
and its people.

Debt is owed to Black people for centuries of merciless
treatment, mendacious
reordering of the historical record and torturous
psychic damage.

Debt is owed for systematically stealing the cultural
memory from African people, for
the denaturing and renaming them thereby
creating a people unaware of

themselves and whose history and person is now
synonymous with slavery and slave.

The successful creation of the "Negro" people in the United States is the
tortuous American tragedy. This white supremacist metaphor started in this
land with the ethnic cleansing and genocide of American indigenous people,
renamed Indians and/or Native Americans. Thereby, let it be stated
forcefully and without doubt or hesitation that the United States was founded
and developed on two genocides, that of the indigenous people and that of
the enslaved Africans. Now, today, in this new century and millennium it is
documented, confirmed and agreed upon by all thinking and well meaning
people that—

Debt is owed to First Nations People and Black people forced:
to laugh when there is nothing funny,
to smile when they are in pain,
to demean themselves on stage, in film, television and
videos,
to dance when their hearts hurt,
to accept delusion as truth,
to lie to their children in the face of contradiction,
to pray to a God that does not look like them,
to pay compounded interest on the wealth they
          created,
to sell their souls for acceptance in a fairy tale,
to mortgage their spirits for another people's history,
to support white peoples-affirmative action with
centuries of Black labor, intelligence and taxes
to create America's music and be denied the fortunes
          made for others,
to see clearly and act as if they are blind,
to act stupid in the eyes of a fearful rulership,
to say yes when they really mean No!
to go into battle to maim or kill other Blacks, whites
          and non-whites,
          for the benefit of whites.

What does America owe First Nations "Indians" and
        Black people?
What is the current worth of America? Or
count the stars in all of the galaxies and multiply in
        dollars by 100 billion,
for a reflective start.

ALWAYS REMEMBER WHERE YOU ARE

1.
it seems as though she had been
planted outside northwestern high
next to the basketball court on 86th street
behind her weather-worn blue buick
seated on a rusting folding
chair where she sold cookies, candies, history,
causes, chewing gum, vision, corn chips,
soda pop and advice to teenagers with
26-year-old mothers and grandmothers
under 40. Most of their father's music
ceased during vietnam and the fbi's
war against black men who dared to
question the saintliness of congress and the
imperial presidency.

2.
she sold wisdom from her weather
worn buick bought for her by her son,
a former NBA basketball star. he had
earned NBA records and money in new york
during the 60s and 70s flying high above
hoops and reality only to slip on a
nickel bag and later fall into deadly
habit of sniffing his breakfast, lunch
and dinner, eventually his snacks interrupted
practice and games as his place in
the world became that of a certified
junky circling a basketball that
he could not bounce and a mother
he could not recognize, nor she him.

3.
as his records faded and his money
disappeared quicker than shit in
a flushing toilet, he returned home to

mama, a pitiful casualty, unable
to write his name or remember the
love that got him out of dusable high
with scholarship offers from 50
universities, no questions asked.
that his mother cared and he was 1st team
all american high school and college is
now history. this mother, in the august
and winter of her time, with eyes
and smile frozen in urban memories,
sells sugar and dreams now from the
trunk of destroyed promises in america.

for Zora Neale Hurston

ART: A Comment

the summer & winter beauty
of a people's culture rides
heroically in their arts.
study human creation for the secrets to
killers & saints,
fools & wise speakers.
search their music for heartbeat,
         their drama for recall and tomorrows,
         their literature for will and vision,
         their visualforms for uncluttered love and
         mountains.
the art makers
those tenacious forgers of truth
are hungry for your smile,
they know in america that plastic & soaps are in,
that the cry is sameness in the skyscrapers and
the captive form is to defeat flowers
& strap concrete to ideas
while pursuing relationships that would
embarrass babies.
among the new & few
it is accepted that art exposes
rats in the crib,
clowns in the temple,
idiots in the congress,
rot in the wheat.
art provides the beat the tellin heat the ellington
         bounce
wright's anger brooks' hook dunham's glide the
         feelings' feel & field.
the rounded callin cards
washing change in the city,
fightin suffocation & money looking for investments
         are
visionaries claiming elegant & ugly.
artist

do not seek immortality
seek ears & eyes   minds & conformation
seek smiles in the young change in the motion
& are aware of harm in daylight and of nations
planning cross cultural trips to africa
while simultaneously implanting your image on
          postage stamps.

*Remembering Murry DePillars, Jeff Donaldson, Babatunde,
Graves, Jon Lockard, Floyd Coleman and the enlightened
work of Bing Davis and the National Conference of Artists.*

JOURNEY CONFIRMED

your furniture has seen the sunrise
in chicago, south of bronzeville in a home
made by alice, a visionary, worker, warm
mother on a mission to see her children grow in a wonderless world
made by enemies of climate and facts,
lovers of concrete, guns, billboards, war and not you.

enter the history of christian slaveholders and rapists,
enter the leadership of quantum liars, fabricators and flash fiction:
creators of students' debt, plastic-card credit and pleonectic oligarchy
and plutocracy resulting in same-same consumers searching for solutions
in big-boxed-stores, tv worship, internet and big pharma killer pills.

in these days where acknowledged wisdom is questioned,
denied, ridiculed and reduced to 280-character tweets
on phones made in china, taiwan and not america.
there exists political cowardice, supreme confusion, doubt, fear
and blame-the-others rulership. missing is
silence, deep reading and knowledge acquisition
where the sacred is embraced, shared and built upon.

enter the music of concentrated learning and alphabets.
our people are melody creators, hand farmers and green producers,
food architects, god talkers, believers in earth, sun, life of water
in a time of corrupted corruption. we are not graveyard people
buying into the senseless acts of uncaring ignorance,
authorized falsehoods, me-tooism and academic clown-talk.
on this day in the south of indiana we soar with this man,
an earth traveler with a smile, a listener to all languages,
the bringer of complicated questions, foreign students,
reverberated kindness and knowledge searched.
this man elevated to be the entrance to the hearts, minds, dreams,
journeys of sentences and paragraphs seeking young people destined
to claim tomorrow's tomorrow in the open doors of this house of knowledge.
where *why* is the beginning of yes, to be led
by a 'we' educator secure in his homegrown brilliance

and open-door deliverances. he walks with a breath view of the sea
for all young voyagers, advocating and encouraging
their safe passages into the magic of brainwork,
decision-making, intricate writing and thinking,
blooming endnotes and the real wealth of
book learning—all becoming the answers.

welcome Dr. Ronald S. Rochon, a clarion voice,
advanced thinker, range-finder, stair-climber,
hands on mentor, son of Africa and America
with feet, mind, body, family and yeses firmly grounded
as the Fourth President of the University of Southern Indiana.

welcome to truth be told, accepted, and confirmed.
ashe, ashe, ashe

for Lynn Rochon

PERFECT BUILDER, QUIET HURRICANE: Beverly Lomax

with her uniquely studied and
quilted mind, her artistically created
home of peace, presence and perfectly
passionate love, there is also an understanding of
sun tzu's *The Art of War*. she, a mosaic quiet reader of
under-notes with sound knowledge of the
unsaid and the clearly unseen attached to
her mathematical mind thinking 24/7
subsurface for solutions. her rich smile issues in
laughter and commitment from the most battle tested doubters.
her life's activity is "we can do this," delivers
critical warmth in a spiritually, community voice of
insight, intellect and non-judgement.
she acknowledges that our children are wounded,
     from birth it is color,
                    it is the hair,
                    it becomes the way we talk,
                    walk, bounce to music and drums and
view the world as possibilities with danger, potholes,
dirty snow, killer rain, wrong names and
false christianity. yet quietly, she finds moments of beauty,
minutes of yes to our history of the unanswered. having studied
the algebra of the human heart she is decidedly visible and continues
awakening the future in the least of us, the often forgotten.
she too, is our bright answer and example always on call,
as grandmother, educator, quilt designer, sociologist and carpenter doing the
necessary work.

for Walter P. Lomax, Jr. and children

HE NEVER SAW THE BULLETS COMING

I.   born in a time of war

there is little memory of
denmark vessey and those who betrayed him
nat turner's revolt centuries before the turner diaries
harriet tubman and the fear her name evoked
sojourner truth and people running from her words,
frederick douglass refusing to accept whiplash
marcus garvey daring to organize millions of Black people
without the permission of whites, w. e. b. du bois
committed to thinking outside the box, circle
and lies of white conquerors. ida b. wells
challenging the real fake news. elijah muhammad's
confirmation of Black as integral to self-definition
and giving malcolm x a voice.
fred hampton daring to tell the people the truth
about their lives decades before black lives
mattered, in a time, as is today, where white lives
matter more as anti-democracy movements entrenched themselves.

II.   betrayal of one's own kind

it is the wisdom of children that is missing
from the blue notes of Black musicians who were
always ahead, not knowing it themselves,
as we revolutionaries pushed, shoved, made up new languages
that closely approximated our over needed call for meaningful
resolution, light quest, love, honor, and yeses from our creator
by conditions forced into our singular lives within the watchful eyes
of the enemies, the enemies of art, drum making and almond milk

the night before the hunt and kill—they laughed.
the negro officers renewed their nigger cards,
the white officers dipped their bullets in pig oil, and
tore up the constitution, bill of rights and

proclaimed that god is white-white, and we go
before first light with orders from washington
chicago's kill squad and fbi's COINTELPRO.
reporters who really wanted to be poets
confronted their contradictory truths which ate
their eyes and minds and burned their fingernails off
while they choked on their lying tongues

it was murder.
& we meet to hear the speeches/ the same, the duplicators.
they say that which is expected of them.
to be instructive or constructive is to be unpopular (like: the
leaders only
sleep when there is a watchingeye)
but they say the right things at the right time, it's like a
stageshow:
only the entertainers have changed.
we remember bobby hutton. the same, the duplicators.

the seeing eye should always see.
the night doesn't stop the stars
& our enemies scope the ways of blackness in three bad
shifts a day.
in the AM their music becomes deadlier.
this is a game of dirt.

only Blackpeople play it fair.

*Commissioned by Chicago magazine recognizing the 50th Anniversary
of the assassination of Fred Hampton on December 4th 1969.*

CONSUMED BY THE IDEA OF A LIBERATED PEOPLE

ignorance always wins
in the century's long white dismissal of a people
in the largeness of white-rimmed colorful hats
of a Sunday-go-to-meetings-people whose understanding
of the why and where of us is limited to tomorrows' tomorrow
whose language of us is defined in other people's ideas, books and deeds.
whose misreading of their created negroes
forever falsely diagnosed and medicated,
ill-framed, ill-treaded, stolen from and blamed for their own
enslavement, seasoning, and acculturated sources of failures.
we cannot dismiss 6,000 years of the afterthoughts
of alien plunder, abduction, theft & translations
of their reality imposed on the world.

ignorance always wins
in a people's inability to heal and experience
clean air, drinkable water, fertile land, self-definition,
unfiltered knowledge, mobility, Black thinking
and acting upon dreams that work for children, Black children
feeling safe, loved and able to see beyond "shake your money maker."
we have always been a foreign language to others
making choices in the prisons of enemies' decisions.

where white lives matter more, more and more
creating worlds of "sluggish Black minds, guilty Black conscience,
treacherous Black hands and shuffling Black feet."
educated by ignorant people talking and writing about how ignorant
other people are, most living in their many seasons
of Black self-contempt and Black denial.

enter African people: diop, clarke, wells, bethune, du bois, nkrumah, nzinga,
          washington, morrison, bearden, williams, white, baldwin, wright,
          malcolm, brooks, randall, b. wright, carruthers, thompson
          and the millions undercounted who rejected betrayal, trinkets and
          white supremacist lies and toys.

enter Black scholars and artists' interpreting original documents, willing to risk all
        for the love of Black people,
enter developers of Black historiography of retelling, original viewing and smiles,
enter the communiversity of yeses to us and those seeking the rightness and
    complexity of us.

there was a time among us when genius was recognized, recorded, rewarded, pro-
tected and listened to. There was a time when Black genius knew what
    we didn't know
and informed the least of us of what we needed to know.

ashe ashe ashe

for Anderson Thompson

EXPECTATIONS HIGH:
LeBron Builds I Promise School While Talking & Dribbling

people Black and stone
be careful that which is designated beautiful
most of us have been taught from the basements
of other peoples' minds.
often we mistake strip mining for farming
and that which truly glows is swept under
the rug of group production, greed, and fame.
it is accepted in america that beauty is
thin, long, and the color of bubblegum.
few articles generated by the millions are beautiful
except people.

trust people
one by one
the darker they come
the more you give your heart,
their experiences most likely are yours
or will be yours
even within the hue & hueless
among them are those
who have recently lost their
ability to recall, listen or feel.

they can hurt you
drop you to your knees with words
that contribute abundantly to Black unknowing,
much of that which blasts from their mouths
is not them   the offense is
they do not know that it is not them
ignorance magnified,
as they rip your heart open
and reduce you to the enemy.

as our authentic enemies
centuries upon us visible and deadly
suffocate our souls, appropriate our language and wordplay,
bastardize our music, dehumanize our unique
essence, caricature our dance, walk and dress
who remain fanatically in awe of Black presence:
on football fields, running tracks, basketball courts, baseball diamonds,
tennis courts, golf courses, soccer fields, legal avenues, entertainment stages,
streets, bedrooms, study halls, military and beyond.
they without guilt or any pretense of fairness
continuously wage holy war against equity
& justice for deep colored people.

yet and yet,
intimately known to the least and left out of us
that the best way to
effectively fight an
alien culture
is to live your own.

for Savannah James & students of the I Promise School

GRANDFATHERS: They Speak Through Me

for W.E.B. Du Bois and Paul Robeson

His father's father prepared him to bite his tongue,
power-listening became his gateway to information
and race knowledge,
his mother's father embraced him fully with large hugs and
words of "can-do" possibilities
in a time of darkness and treachery.
i was their blood mixture, their bone,
their claim to immortality and song.

grandfather graves declared white
people deficient, diseased and dangerous,
he had scars documenting it, he,
an african-black laborer could fix anything
moving that had a motor, a self-taught mechanic
who was gang beaten at 22 for correcting a white man at a
chevy dealership during a time when the accepted
attitude in arkansas for negroes in the presence
of whites was head bowed, eyes deep to the ground. quiet.
defeated.

grandfather lee a bronze colored
detroit minister of the baptist persuasion
never worked a day for white folks, god talked to him early
and he kept his smile.
he pastored to a community where eyes and work seldom said
no or "can't do," starting from a storefront growing into a
used movie theatre, to building from the earth up,
into a 1,500-seat stained glass, concrete and fine wood
cathedral, this became an answer.
god was his mission, his people his melody
and neither *quit* nor *quiet* were in him.
he anchored bronzeville, negotiated with white stones, had
what his congregation called good back-up, the solid feed of
osun, obatala, and shango.

at six i was at their knees consuming words, jerks,
silences and secrets.
at eleven i was taken to the woods and left with knife, water
and a map, manhood was coming. soon.
at thirteen i was taken to the pulpit,
given the bible, songbook and silver watch,
jesus was in the air and always on time.
at fourteen i discovered richard wright, louis
armstrong, chester himes, miles davis, langston hughes,
gwendolyn brooks and motown. i was branded crazy, insolent
and world-wounded for the question i asked and for the
burn in my eyes.
as a young man i carried many knowledges,
ran between two cultures
cleared my head between the military and the libraries
and cried for the loss of my mother.
i kissed girls and black politics on the g.i. bill in college and
was exiled into black struggle in the early sixties.
i learned to ride the winds of battle.

as a man i chose poetry, love and extended family.
i selected black independence, institution building and
the cherry eyes of children as my mission.
i breathe the smoke and oxygen from the fires of my
          grandfathers,
i have their slow smile, quick mind and necessary wit, i wear
their earth shoes and dance with their languages,

i speak in the cadences of southern trees,
holy water and books,
i carry their messages and courageous hearts,
my eyes are ancestor deep, bold and intrepid,
i whisper their songs as mantras.
my music is accelerated blues, the four tops and trane.
it is they, my grandfathers who taught me the notes and
rhythms and as the son of

#WECANTBREATHE:
The Misrule of the True Enemy of the State: Forty-Five

A Poet's Witness to a Catastrophe

forty-five's election and presidency was/is dependent upon
his lies, double & triple lies (over 20,000 in less than four years),
his con game fabrications & falsifications,
his maximization and abuse of mass & social media,
his thousands of millionaire & billionaire enablers, his gifts
for marketing racist white nationalism and white supremacy
as normal and aspirational to his followers and the nation, all
bolstered by *jane crow* white women, the republican party
and white evangelical anti-christian christians. his incompetence
and executive actions are a human virus and plague on the world
eliciting national trauma, unearned suffering & self-doubt.
forty-five is the first president in modern politics to openly, brazenly
brag about / grab the pussy / and an in-your-face "fence them in"
disrespect and belittling of women, especially Black, Brown, First Nation and
Asian.
at this hypercritical time in the lives of our children, forty-five has embraced
baby caging, masklessness, non-reading, non-studying and non-thinking
as badges of border defense, medical expertise, fascism & lie talk,
thereby, the tweeter-in-chief has nationally set in motion anti-intellectual
policies in the white house and most republican centers of influence.
to young people wishing to use language and nuanced narratives as a force
of good, i.e., as teachers, journalists, writers, medical workers, historians,
scientists, mathematicians, and god forbid poets, who all trust in writing
and publishing to define themselves and the planet. we now live in
the abyss and universe of aggressive autocrats, the NRA & fear achievers
surrounding a nasty chief executive and his cabinet of thieves reordering
our lives: multitudes of cowards, family members and grifters serving
the dear leader. his crime family and extended family who'd rather bark
like dogs, watch 24/7/365 rupert murdoch's Fox counterfactual news
and gleefully legitimize the exaggerated and misleading hatred of the other.
the others who forty-five blames for all the ills of the world as ignorant
people supporting him talk about how ignorant other people are;
where "fewer people have more" and the majority of us are caught between

an earthquake and hurricane in fighting to survive and thrive in the myth
of *american exceptionalism* led by "a very stable genius," actively seeking
the destruction of public education, US post office, social security,
Obamacare,
Black voting, unions and democracy. needed immediately & yesterday
are enlightened, intelligent, open-minded and faithfully committed
women and men of all cultures and classes to get in "good trouble"
to not break bread with the devil and his kind, but to redefine
for their children and all of us a world that must move with turbo speed
toward the creation of Martin Luther King, Jr.'s Beloved community.

for Ella Baker, John Lewis and C. T. Vivian

ART

1

Art is a prodigious and primary energy force. Children's active participation in music, dance, painting, poetry and film, photography and the indigenous crafts of their people is what makes them whole, significantly human, secure in their own skin, culture and abilities. Thus, generating in them unlimited possibilities.

Art is fundamental instruction and food for a people's soul as they translate the many languages and acts of becoming, often telling them in no uncertain terms that all humans are not pure or perfect. However, the children of all cultures inherit their creator's capacity to originate from the bone of their imaginations, the closest manifestations of purity, perfection, and beauty. Art, at least, encourages us to walk on water, dance on top of trees and skip from star to star without being able to swim, keep a beat or fly. A child's "on fire" imagination is the one universal prerequisite for becoming an artist.

2

Magnify your children's minds with art,
jumpstart their questions with art,
introduce your children to the cultures of the world
through art,
energize their young feet, spirits and souls with art,
infuse the values important to civil culture via art,
keep them curious, political and creative through art,
speak and define the universal language of
beauty through art,
learn to appreciate peace with art,
approach the cultures of others through their art,
introduce the spiritual paths of other
people through art,

keep young people in school, off drugs and
out of prison with art,
keep their young minds running, jumping
and excited with art.
examine the nurturing moments of love,
peace and connecting differences with art.

3

Art allows and encourages the love of self and others. The best
artists are not mass murderers, criminals or child molesters;
they are in the beauty and creation business. Art is elemental
to intelligent intelligence, working democracy, freedom, equality
and justice. Art, if used wisely and widely, early and often
is an answer and a question. It is the cultural lake that the
indigenous rivers of dance, music, local images and voices
flow. Art is the waterfall of life, reflecting the untimely and
unique soul of a people. Art is the drumbeat of good and great
hearts forever seeking peace and a grand future for all
enlightened peoples. For these are the people the world over
who lovingly proclaim, "give the artists some," kind words,
financial support, yeses from your heart, knowing intuitively
that there will be creative reciprocity in all that they give us.
Why? Because fundamentally art inspires, informs, directs,
generates hope and challenges the receiver to respond.
And finally, and this is consequential, the quality of the art
determines the quality of the responses.

for Gwendolyn Brooks

ALL CHILDREN ARE PRECIOUS

it is not uncommon to see her
in unexpected moments smiling at the loudly impossible.
the great mission in her life is measured
by making believers out of angry experts
who use toilet tissue to write their books and reports
on the largely impossible melodies,
they confirm noise, she hears music

strangers feel that her affection
is illegal but apparent.

her love is a Blackbold quilt
wearing the palm prints of children questioning
the direction of their fingers
the colors in their eyes and extreme ideas.
however, they re not opposing forces
their hearts are consumptive, calm and clear
when caring is present.

our children see the lies and failures in the eyes
of teachers who have given up.
our children survive cultural ignorance, soda pop,
potato chips and sweet cake breakfasts, each other
and people with earned degrees.
what are the ethics of children without self-knowledge?

she sees children as sacred places,
she has a repairable heart and
the quiet word on the street is that
Duke Ellington would have liked her smile.
in it gleams her greatest theme
the love of our children and the articulation of
their possibilities.

for Barbara A. Sizemore, May 9, 1997

ADDENDUM

ON BECOMING ANTI-RAPIST

Haki R. Madhubuti

If we men, of all races, cultures and continents would just examine the inequalities of power in our families, businesses, spiritual and political institutions, and decide today to reassess and reconfigure them in consultation with the women in our lives, we would all be doing the most fundamental corrective act of a counter-rapist.

> there are mobs & strangers
> in us
> who scream of the women
> wanted and
> will get
> as if the women
> are ours for the
> taking.

In 1991, the crime of rape in the United States entered our consciousness with the power of the dissolution of the U.S.S.R. The trials of William Kennedy Smith (of the Camelot family) and Iron Mike Tyson, former heavyweight boxing champion of the entire world, shared front pages and provided talk-show hosts with subject matter on a topic that is usually confined to women's groups and the butt jokes of many men. Since women are over 50% of the world's population and a clear majority in this country, one would think that the question of rape would not still be hidden in the minor concern files of men.

However, what is not hidden is that Mr. Kennedy Smith and Mr. Tyson both tried defenses that blamed the women in question. For Smith that tactic was successful; for Tyson, it failed. Pages of analysis have been written in both cases, and I do not wish to add to them. But one can safely state that no woman wants to be raped, and that if men were raped at the frequency of women, rape would be a federal crime rivaling those of murder and bank robbery. If car-jacking can command federal attention, why are we still treating rape as if it's a "boys will be boys" sport or a woman's problem as in "blame the victim"? In the great majority of sex crimes against women in the United States, women are put on trial as if they planned and executed their own rapes.

Male acculturation (or a better description would be male "seasoning") is anti-female, anti-womanist/feminist, and anti-reason when it comes to women's equal measure and place in society. This flawed socialization of men is not confined to the West but permeates most, if not all, cultures in the modern world. Most men have been taught to treat, respond, listen and react to women from a male's point of view. Black men are not an exception here; we, too, are imprisoned with an intellectual/sexual/spiritual understanding of women based upon antiquated male culture and sexist orientation—or should I say, miseducation. For example, sex or sexuality is hardly ever discussed, debated, or taught to Black men in a nonthreatening or non-embarrassing family or community setting.

Men's view of women, specifically Black women outside of the immediate family, is often one of "bitch," "my woman," "ho," or any number of designations that demean and characterize Black women as less than whole and productive persons. Or missteps toward an understanding of women are compounded by the cultural environments where much of the talk or women takes place: street corners, locker rooms, male clubs, sporting events, bars, military service, business trips, playgrounds, workplaces, basketball courts, etc. Generally, women are not discussed on street corners or in bars as intellectual or culturally compatible partners. Rather the discussion focuses of what is the best way to "screw" or control them.

These are, indeed, learning environments that traditionally are not kind to women. We are taught to see women as commodities and/or objects for men's sexual releases and sexual fantasies; also, most women are considered "inferiors" to men and thus are not to be respected or trusted. Such thinking is encouraged and legitimized by our culture and transmitted via institutional structures (churches, workplaces), mass media (*Playboy* and *Penthouse*), misogynist music (rap and mainstream), and R-rated and horror films that use exploitative images of women. And of course, there are the ever-present, tall, trim, "Barbie-doll" women featured in advertising for everything from condoms to the latest diet "cures." Few men have been taught, really taught, from birth—to the heart, to the gut—to respect, value, or even, on occasion, to honor women. Only until very recently has it been confirmed in Western culture that rape (unwelcomed/uninvited sex) is criminal, evil and antihuman.

our mothers, sisters, wives and
daughters ceased to be the
women men want   we think of them as
loving family   music & soul   bright wonderments.
they are not locker room talk
not the hunted lust or   dirty
cunt burnin hos.
bright wonderments are excluded   by association as
blood & heart   bone & memory
& we will destroy a rapist's knee caps,
& write early grave on his thoughts
to protect them.

Human proximity defines relationships. Exceptions should be noted, but in most cultures and most certainly within the Black/African worldview, family and extended family ties are honored and respected and protected. In trying to get a personal fix here, that is, an understanding of the natural prohibitions against rape, think of one's own personhood being violated. Think of one's own family subjected to this act. Think of the enslavement of African people, it was common to have breeding houses on most plantations where one's great-great-grandmothers were forced to open their insides for the sick satisfaction of white slave owners, overseers, and enslaved Black men.

This forced sexual penetration of African women led to the creation of mixed-raced people here and around the world. There is a saying in South Africa that the colored race did not exist until nine months after white men arrived. This demeaning of Black women and other women is amplified in today's culture, where it is not uncommon for young men to proclaim that "pussy is a penny a pound." However, we are told that such a statement is not meant for one's own mother, grandmother, sister, daughter, aunt, niece, close relative or extended family. Yet, the point must be maid rather emphatically that incest (family rape) is on the rise in this country. Incest between adults and children is often not revealed until the children are adults. At that point their lives are so confused and damaged that many continue incestuous acts.

it will do us large to recall
when the animal in us rises
that all women are someone's
mother, sister, wife or daughter
and are not fruit to be stolen when hungry.

Part of the answer is found in the question: Is it possible or realistic to view all women are precious persons? Selective memory plays an important role here. Most men who rape are seriously ill and improperly educated. They do not view women outside of their "protected zone" as precious blood, do not see them as extended family, and do not see them as individuals or independent persons to be respected as most men respect other men. Mental illness or brain mismanagement blocks out reality, shattering and negating respect for others, especially, the others of which one wishes to take advantage. Power always lurks behind rape. Rape is an act of aggression that asserts power by defaming and defiling. Most men have been taught—either directly or indirectly—to solve problems with force. Such force may be verbal or physical. Violence is the answer that is promoted in media everywhere, from Saturday morning cartoons to everyday television to R-rated films. Popular culture has a way of trivializing reality and confusing human expectations, especially with regard to relationships with men and women. For too many Black people, the popular has been internalized. In many instances, the media define us, including our relationships to each other.

Women have been in the forefront of the anti-rape struggle. Much of this work has taken place in nontraditional employment, such as serving in police and fire departments, as top professors and administrators in higher education, as elected and public servants in politics and in the fields of medicine and law. However, the most pronounced presence and "advancement" of women has been seen in the military. We are told that the military, in terms of social development, remains at the cutting edge of changes, especially in the progress of Blacks and female soldiers. However, according to Gary A. Warner in the *San Francisco Examiner* (December 30, 1992), the occurrence of rape against women in the military is far greater than in civilian life:

> A woman serving in the Army is 50 percent more likely to be raped than a civilian, newly released military records obtained by the Orange County Register show.
>
> From 1981 to 1987, 484 female soldiers were raped while on active duty, according to Department of Army records released after a Freedom of Information Act request.
>
> The Army rate of 129 rape cases per 100,000 population in 1990 exceeds nationwide statistics for the same year compiled by the FBI of 80 confirmed rape cases per 100,000 women. The 1990 statistics are the latest comparable ones available.

The brutality of everyday life continues to confirm the necessity for caring men and women to confront inhuman acts that cloud and prevent wholesome development. Much of what is defined as sexual "pleasure" today comes at the terrible expense of girls and often boys. To walk Times Square of any number of big city playgrounds after dark is to view how loudly the popular throwaway culture has trapped, corrupted and sexually abused too many of our children. In the United States the sexual abuse of runaway children, and children sentenced to foster care and poorly supervised orphanages, is nothing less than scandalous. The proliferation of battered women's shelters and the most recent revelation of the sexual abuse of women incarcerated in the nation's prisons only underscores the prevailing view of women by a substantial number of men, as sex objects for whatever sick acts that enter their minds.

Such abuse of children is not confined to the United States. Ron O' Grady, coordinator of the International Campaign to End Child Prostitution in Asiatic Tourism, fights an uphill battle to highlight the physical and economic maltreatment of children. Murray Kempton reminds us in his essay "A New Colonialism" *(The New York Review of Books,* November 19, 1992) of Thailand's "supermarkets for the purchases of small and disposable bodies." He goes on to state that:

Tourism is central to Thailand's developmental efforts; and the attractions of its ancient culture compare but meagerly to the compelling pull its brothels exercise upon foreign visitors. The government does its duty to the economy by encouraging houses of prostitution and pays its debt to propriety with its insistence that no more than 10,000 children work there. Private observers concerned with larger matters that the good name of public officials estimate for the real total of child prostitutes in Thailand at 200,000.

The hunters and others of children find no border closed. They have ranged into South China carrying television sets to swap one per child. The peasants who cursed the day a useless girl was born know better now; they can sell her for consumers overseas and be consumers themselves. Traffickers less adventurous stay at home and contrive travel agencies that offer cheap trips to Kuala Lumpur that end up with sexual enslavement in Japan or Malaysia.

That this state of affairs is not better known speaks loudly and clearly to the devaluation of female children. The war in Sarajevo, Bosnia, and Herzegovina again highlights the status of women internationally. In the rush toward ethnic cleansing and narrow and exclusive nationalism, Serbian soldiers have been indicted for murder and other war crimes. The story of one such soldier, Borislav Herak, is instructive. According to an article by John F. Burnes in the New York Times (November 27, 1992) entitled "A Serbian Fighter's Trial of Brutality," Mr. Herak and other soldiers were given the go-ahead to rape and kill Muslim women:

> The indictment lists 29 individual murders between June and October, including eight rape-murders of Muslim women held prisoner in an abandoned motel and café outside Vogosca, seven miles north of Sarajevo, where, Mr. Herak said he and other Serbian fighters were encouraged to rape women and then take them away to kill them in hilltops and other deserted places.
> The indictment also covers the case of 220 other Muslim civilians in which Mr. Herak has confessed to being a witness or taking part, many of them women and children. (Also see the January 4, 1993 issue of Newsweek.)

Much in the lives of women is not music or melody but is their dancing to the beat of the unhealthy and often killing drums of men and make teenagers. Rape is not the fault of women; however, in a male-dominated world, the victims are often put on the defensive and forced to rationalize their gender and their personhood.

> Rape is not a reward for warriors
> it is war itself
> a deep, deep tearing, a dislocating of
> the core of the womanself.
> rape rips heartlessly
> soul from spirit,
> obliterating colors from beauty and body
> replacing melody and music with
> rat venom noise and uninterrupted intrusion and beatings.

The brutality of rape is universal. Most modern cultures—European, American, African, Asian, religious and secular—grapple with this crime. Rarely is there discussion, and, more often than not, women are discouraged from being a part of the debates and edits. Rape is cross-cultural. I have not visited, heard of, or read about any rape-free societies. The war against women is international. Daily, around the world, women fight for a little dignity and their earned place in the world. And men in power respond accordingly. For example, Barbara Crossette reported in the *New York Times* (April 7, 1991) about an incident in Batamaloo, Kashmir:

> In this conservative Muslim society, women have moved to the forefront of demonstrations and also into guerilla conclaves. No single event has contributed more to this rapidly rising militancy among women than reports of a gang rape months ago by Indian troops in Kunan, a remote village in northwestern Kashmir.
>
> According to a report filed by S.M. Yasin, district magistrate in Kupwara, the regional center, the armed forces "behaved like violent beasts." He identified them as members of the fourth Rajputana Rifles and said that they rampaged through the village from 11 P.M. on Feb. 23 until 9 the next morning.
>
> "A large number of armed personnel entered into the houses of villagers and at gun-point they gang raped 23 ladies, without any consideration go their age, married, unmarried, pregnancy etc.," he wrote. "There was a hue and cry in the whole village." Local people say that as many as 100 women were molested in some way.

As a man of African descent, I would like to think that Africans have some special insight, enlightened hearts, or love in us that calms us in such times of madness. But my romanticism is shattered everyday as I observe Black communities across this land. The number of rapes reported an unreported in our communities is only the latest and most painful example of how far we have drifted from beauty. However, it is seldom that I have hurt more than when I learned about the "night of terror" that occurred in Meru, Kenya on July 13, 1991, at the St. Kizito boarding school. A high school protest initiated by the boys, in which the girls refused to join, resulted in a night of death, rapes and beatings unparalleled in modern Kenya, in Africa or in the world. As Timothy Dryer reported in the *Chicago Tribune* (April 18, 1991):

In Kenya, one-party rule has resulted in a tyranny of the majority. Dissent, even in politics is not welcome. "Here, the minority always must go along with the majority's wishes," said a businessman who has done a lot of work with the government in the last 15 years and asked not to be named. "And it is said that a woman cannot say no to a man."

Women's groups have said the rapes and deaths were an extreme metaphor for what goes on in the Kenyan society. The girls of St. Kizito dared to say no to the boys, and 19 paid with their lives while 71 others were beaten and raped....

There have been many school protests in Kenya this year. This summer alone, some 20 protests have turned into riots resulting in the destruction of school property. There have been rapes at other schools when girls have refused to join boys in their protests.

A growing part of the answer is that we men, as difficult as it may seem, must view all women (race, color, religion or nationality aside) as extended family. The question is, and I know that I am stretching: Would we rape our mothers, grandmothers, sisters or other female relatives, or even give such acts a thought? Can we extend this attitude to all women? Therefore, we must:

1. Teach our sons that it is their responsibility to be anti-rapist; that is, they must be counter-rapist in thought, conversations, raps, organizations and actions.
2. Teach our daughters how to defend themselves and maintain an uncompromising stance toward men and boys.
3. Understand that being a counter-rapist is honorable, manly, and necessary for a just society.
4. Understand that anti-rapist actions are part of the Black tradition; being an anti-rapist is in keeping with the best African culture and with African family and extended family configurations. Even in times of war, we were known to honor and respect the personhood of children and women.
5. Be glowing examples of men who are fighting to treat women as equals and to be fair and just in associations with women. This means at the core that families as now defined and constructed must continually be reassessed. In today's economy, most women, married

and unmarried, must work. We men must encourage them in their work and must be intimately involved in rearing children and doing homework.

6. Understand that just as men are different from one another, women also differ, therefore, we must try not to stereotype women into the limiting and often debilitating expectations of men. We must encourage and support them in their searching and development.

7. Be unafraid of independent, intelligent, and self-reliant women. And by extension, understand that intelligent women think for themselves and may not want to have sex with a particular man. This is a woman's prerogative and is not a comment on anything else other than the fact that she does not want to have sex.

8. Be bold and strong enough to stop other men (friends or strangers) from raping and to intervene in a rape in process with the fury and destruction of a hurricane against the rapist.

9. Listen to women, Listen to women, especially to womanist/feminist/ Pan-Africanist philosophies of life. Also, study, the writings of women, especially Black women.

10. Act responsibly in response to the listening and studying. Be a part of and support anti-rape groups for boys and men. Introduce-anti-rape discussion into men's groups and organizations.

11. Never stop growing and understand that growth is limited and limiting without the input of intelligent women.

12. Learn to love. Study love. Even if one is at war, love and respect, respect and love must conquer, if there is to be a sane and lovable world. Rape is anti-love and anti-respect. Love is not easy. One does not fall into love but grows into love.

We can put to rest the rape problem in one generation if its eradication is as important to us as our cars, jobs, careers, sport-games, beer and quest for power. However, the women who put rape on the front burners must continue to challenge us and their own cultural training, and position themselves so that they and their messages are not compromised or ignored.

a significant few of their
fathers, brothers, husbands, sons
and growing strangers
are willing to unleash harm on the earth

and spill blood in the eyes
of
maggots in running shoes
who do not know the sounds of birth
or respect the privacy of the human form.

If we are to be just in our internal rebuilding, we must challenge tradition and cultural ways of life that relegate women to inferior status in the home, church/mosque/temple, workplace, political life and education. Men are not born rapists; we are taught very subtly, often in unspoken ways, that women are ours for the taking. Generally, such teachings begin with the family. Enlightenment demands fairness, impartiality, and vision; it demands confrontation of outdated definitions and acceptance of fair and just resolutions. One's sex, race, social class or wealth should not determine entitlements or justice. If we are honest, men must be in the forefront of eradicating sex stereotypes in all facets of private and public life. I think that being honest, as difficult and as self-incriminating as it may be, is the only way that we can truly liberate ourselves. If men can liberate themselves (with the help of women) from the negative aspects of the culture that produced them, maybe a just, fair, good and liberated society is possible in our lifetime.

The liberation of the male psyche from preoccupation of domination, power hunger, control and absolute rightness requires an honest and fair assessment of patriarchal culture. This requires commitment to deep study combined with a willingness for painful, uncomfortable, and often shocking change. We are not where we should be. This is why rape exists; why families are so easily formed and just as easily dissolved; why children are confused and abused; why our elderly is discarded, abused and exploited; and why teenage boys create substitute families (gangs) that terrorize their own communities.

I remain and optimistic realist, primarily because I love life and most of what it has to offer. I often look at my children and tears come to my eyes because I realize how blessed I am to be their father. My wife and the other women in my life are special because they know they are special and have taken it upon themselves, at great cost, to actualize their dreams, making what is considered for many of them unthinkable a few years ago a reality today. If we men, of all races, cultures, and continents would just examine the inequalities of power in our own families, businesses, and political and spiritual institutions, and decide today to reassess and reconfigure them in consultation with women in our lives, we would all be doing the most fundamental corrective act of a counter-rapist.

It is indeed significant, and not an arbitrary aside, that males and females are created biologically different. These profound differences are partially why we are attracted to each other and are also what is beautiful about life. But too often due to hierarchical and patriarchal definitions one's sex also relegates one to a position in life that is not necessarily respected. Sex should not determine moral or economical worth, as it now does in too many cultures. In a just society, one's knowledge and capabilities, that is, what one is actually able to contribute to the world, is more valuable than whether or not the person is male or female.

Respect for the woman closest to us can give us the strength and knowledge to confront the animal in us with regard to the women we consider "others." Also, keep in mind that the "others" often are the women closest to us. If we honestly confront the traditions and histories that have shaped us, we may come to the realization that women should be encouraged to go as far as their intellect and talents will take them—burdened only by the obstacles that affect all of us. Most certainly the sexual energies of men must be checked before our misguided maleness manifests itself in the most horrible of crimes—rape.

No!
Means No!
even when men think
that they are "god's gift to women"
even after dropping a week's check & more
on dinner by the ocean,
the four tops, temptations and intruders memory tour,
imported wine & rose that captured her smile,
suggested to you private music & low lights
drowning out her unarticulated doubts.

Question the thousand years teachings
crawling through your lower depths and
don't let your little head
out think your big head.
No! means No!
even when her signals suggest yes.

LUCILLE CLIFTON: Warm Water, Greased Legs and Dangerous Poetry

Let there be new flowering
in the fields let the fields
turn mellow for the men
let the men keep tender
through the time let the time
be wrested from the war
let the war be won
let love he
at the end[1]

In everything she creates, this Lucille Clifton, a writer of no ordinary substance, a singer of faultless ease and able storytelling, there is a message. No slogans or billboards, but words that are used refreshingly to build us, make us better, stronger, and whole. Words that defy the odds and in the end, make us wiser. Lucille Clifton, unfortunately, is not a household name. Of her twenty published books (four adult, sixteen juvenile), the best read of our people might have difficulty naming two titles. Although they are published by major publishers (Random House for her poetry), one has not seen the types of media publicity we come to expect for an author of her ability and stature.

Lucille Clifton is a woman of majestic presence, a full-time wife, over time mother, part-time street activist and writer of small treasures (most of her books are small but weighty). That she is not known speaks to, I feel, her preoccupation with truly becoming a full Black woman and writer. Celebrity—that is, people pointing you out in drugstores and shopping malls-does not seem to interest her. When she was almost assured of becoming the poet laureate of Maryland, she wrote Gwendolyn Brooks (poet laureate of Illinois) asking if she should consider such a position. I suggest that she really wanted to know: (1) Are there any advantages in the position for her people? and (2) Would she significantly have to change her life by accepting the honor? Brooks' response was, "It is what you make of it." Clifton accepted.

CULTURE AND CONSCIOUSNESS

The city of Baltimore, where she and her family reside, does not figure heavily in her work. The "place" of her poetry and prose is essentially urban landscapes that are examples of most Black communities in this country. Clifton's urge is to live, is to conquer oppressive and nonnatural spaces. Her poetry is often a conscious, quiet introduction to the real world of Black sensitivities. Her focus and her faces are both the men and the women connected and connecting; the children, the family, the slavelike circumstances, the beauty, and the raw and most important the hideouts of Black people to Black people.

Her poetry is emotion-packed and musically fluent to the point of questioning whether a label on it would limit one's understanding. Her first book of poetry, *Good Times* (1969), cannot be looked upon as simply a "first" effort. The work is unusually compacted and memory-evoking.

There is no apology for the Black condition. There is an awareness and a seriousness that speaks to "houses straight as/dead men."2 Clifton's poems are not vacant lots; the mamas and daddies are not forgotten human baggage to be made loose of and discarded. Much of today's writing, especially much of that being published by Black women writers, seems to invalidate Black men or make small of them, often relegating them to the position of white sexual renegades in Black faces.

No such cop-out for Clifton. There is no misrepresentation of the men or women. And one would find it extremely difficult to misread Clifton. She is not a "complicated" writer in the traditional Western sense. She is a writer of complexity, and she makes her readers work and think. Her poetry has a quiet force without being pushy or alien. Whether she is cutting through family relationships, surviving American racial attitudes, or just simply renewing love ties, she puts something heavy on your mind. The great majority of her published poetry is significant. At the base·of her work is concern for the Black family, especially the destruction of its youth. Her eye is for the uniqueness of our people, always concentrating on the small strengths that have allowed us to survive the horrors of Western life.

Her treatment of Black men is unusually significant and sensitive. I feel that part of the reason she treats men fairly and with balance in her work is due to her relationship with her father, brothers, husband, and sons. Generally, positive relationships produce positive results.

my daddy's fingers move among the couplers
chipping steel and skin
and if the steel would break
my daddy's fingers might be men again. [*G.T.*, p. 3]

Lucille Clifton is often calling for the men to be Black men. Asking and demanding that they seek and be more than expected. Despite her unlimited concern for her people, she does not box herself into the comer of preaching at them or of describing them with metaphors of belittlement. Clifton has a fine, sharp voice pitched to high C and tuned carefully to the frequency of the Black world. She is a homeland technician who has not allowed her "education" to interfere with her solos.

The women of *Good Times* are strong and Dahomey-made, are imposing and tragic, yet givers of love. Unlike most of us, Clifton seemed to have taken her experiences and observations and squeezed the knowledge from them, translating them into small and memorable lessons:

. . . surrounded by the smell
of too old potato peels
. . .
you wet brown bag of a woman
who used to be the best looking gal in Georgia
used to be called the Georgia Rose
I stand up
through your destruction
I stand up [G.T., p. 5]

Standing up is what *Good Times* is about. However, Clifton can beat you up with a poem; she can write history into four stanzas and bring forth reaction from the most hardened nonreader. Listen to the story of Robert:

Was born obedient
without questions

did a dance called
Picking grapes
Sticking his butt out
for pennies

Married a master
who whipped his head
until he died
until he died
the color of his life
was nigger. [G.T., p. 6]

There is no time frame in such a poem. Such poems do not date easily. Robert is 1619 and 1981, is alive and dying on urban streets, in rural churches and corporate offices. "Niggers" have not disappeared; some of them (us) are now being called by last names and are receiving different types of mind whippings, mind whippings that achieve the same and sometimes greater results.

Clifton is a Black cultural poet. We see in her work a clear transmission of values. It is these values that form the base of a developing consciousness of struggle. She realizes that we do have choices that can still be exercised. Hers is most definitely to fight. From page to page, from generation to generation, the poems cry out direction, hope, and future. One of the best examples of this connecting force is from her book *An Ordinary Woman* (1974); the poem is "Turning."

Turning into my own
turning on in
to my own self
at last
turning out of the
lady cage
turning at last
on a stem like a black fruit in my own season
at last. [*A.O. w.;* p. 63]

It is the final voyage into oneself that is the most difficult. Then there comes the collective fight, the dismantling of the real monsters outside. But first we must become whole again. The true undiluted culture of a people is the base of wholeness. One way toward such wholeness is what Stephen Henderson calls "saturation," the giving and defining of Blackness through proclaiming such experiences as legitimate and necessary, whereas the Black poetic experience used often enough becomes natural and expected. Clifton "saturates" us in a way that forces us to look at ourselves in a different and more profound way.

For every weakness, she points to a strength; where there are negatives, she pulls and searches for the positives. She has not let the low ebbs of life diminish her talents or toughness. She is always looking for the good, the best, but not naïvely so. Her work is realistic and burning with the energy of renewal.

THE LANGUAGE

Clifton is an economist with words; her style is to use as few words as possible. Yet, she is effective because, despite consciously limiting her vocabulary, she has defined her audience. She is not out to impress, or to showcase the scope of her lexicon. She is communicating ideas and concepts. She understands that precise communication is not an easy undertaking; language, at its root, seeks to express emotion, thought, action. Most poetry writing (other than the blues) is foreign to the Black community. It is nearly impossible to translate to the page the changing linguistic nuances or the subtleties of body language Blacks use in everyday conversation; the Black writer's task is an extremely complicated and delicate one. But understand me, Clifton does not write down to us, nor is she condescending or patronizing with her language. Most of her poems are short and tight, as is her language. Her poems are well-planned creations, and as small as some of them are, they are not cloudy nor rainy with words for words' sake. The task is not to fill the page with letters but to challenge the mind:

What I remember about that day
is boxes stacked across the walk
and couch springs curling through the air
and drawers and tables balanced on the curb
and us, hollering,
leaping up and around
happy to have a playground
nothing about the emptied rooms
nothing about the emptied family [G.T., p. 7]

Her originality is accomplished with everyday language and executed with musical percussion, pushed to the limits of poetic possibilities. Lucille Clifton is a lover of life, a person who feels her people. Her poems are messages void of didacticism and needless repetition. Nor does she shout or scream the language at you; her voice is birdlike but loud and high enough to pierce the ears of dogs. She is the quiet warrior, and, like the weapons of all good warriors, her weapons can hurt, kill, and protect.

Language is the building block of consciousness. To accurately understand the soul of a people, you not only search for their outward manifestations (e.g., institutions, art, science and technology, social and political systems), but you examine their language. And since the Black community, by and large, speaks a foreign language, the question is to what extent have we made the language work for us, i.e., build for us? All languages to some degree are bastards, created by both rulers and the ruled, kings and proletariat, masters and slaves, citizens and visitors. The greatness and endurance of a people to a large degree lies in their fundamental ability to create under the most adverse conditions using the tools at hand. Language is ever growing and a tool (weapon) that must be mastered if it is to work for us.

Language used correctly (communicating and relating at the highest) expands the brain, increases one's knowledge bank, enlarges the world, and challenges the vision of those who may not have a vision. *One of the most effective ways to keep a people enslaved, in a scientific and technological state which is dependent upon a relatively high rate of literacy, is to create in that people a disrespect and fear of the written and spoken word.* For any people to compete in the new world order that is emerging, it is absolutely necessary that study, research, and serious appraisal of documentation that impact people's lives become second nature. Fine poetry is like a tuning fork: it regulates, clears, and challenges the brain, focusing it and bringing it in line with the rest of the world. Therefore, it is a political act to keep people ignorant. We can see that it is not by accident that Black people in the United States watch more television than any other ethnic group and that more of our own children can be seen carrying radios and cassettes to school than books. The point is that it is just about impossible to make a positive contribution to the world if one cannot read, write, compute, think and articulate one's thoughts. The major instrument for bringing out the genius of any people is the productive, creative, and stimulating use and creation of language.

Lucille Clifton has expanded the use of small language. Very seldom does she use words larger than four syllables. She has shaped and jerked, patched and stitched everyday language in a way that few poets have been able to do. In her book *An Ordinary Woman* she fulfills her promise of greatness. The book is a statement of commitment and love. The songs are those that stretch us, and in this final hour mandate the people immortal. Her nationalism is understated, yet compelling, with short stanzas and fistlike lines.

The imposing images in *An Ordinary Woman* are bones. Bones are used as the connecting force of Black people. The word is used fourteen times in a multitude of ways throughout the volume. The image is profoundly effective because bones represent strength ("We will wear/new bones again") (*A.O.W.*, p. 17) and *deep hurt* ("and you Adrienne / broken like a bone" [*A.O.W.*, p. 13]). Bones are secrets ("she / knows places in my bones / I never sing about" [*A.O. W.*, p. 47]); they are closeness and gifts ("and give you my bones / and my blood to feed on" [*A.O.W.*, p. 57]): ever present music ("I beg my bones to be good but / they keep clicking music"[*A.O.W.*, p. 61]). The bones are connectors and death, lineage and life.

> More than once
> I have taken the bones you hardened and built daughters
> and they blossom and promised fruit
> like African trees. [*A.O.W.*, p. 45]

She is what John Gardner describes as the moral writer and what Addison Gayle, Jr., refers to as a writer's writer in the Black nationalist tradition: "The Black writer at the present time must forgo the assimilationist tradition and re-direct his (her) art to the strivings within . . . to do so, he (she) must write for and speak to the majority of Black people; not to a sophisticated elite fashioned out to the programmed computers of America's largest universities.[3]

Clifton's nationalism is sometimes subtle and bright, sometimes coarse and lonely; it is fire and beaten bodies, but what most emerges from the body of her work is a reverence for life, a hope for tomorrow, and an undying will to live and to conquer oppressive forces.

By customary standards she is no ordinary woman. In another time and place, that might have been the case, but here in never-never land, the make-believe capital of the world, she exemplifies the specialness we all need to be. How-ever, the ordinariness she speaks of is an in-group definition between sister and sister:

> me and you be sisters
> we be the same.
> me and you
> coming from the same place. [*A.O.W.*, p. 5]

She, too, is the mother who has had sons and brothers, uncles and male friends, and seems to have learned a great deal from these relationships. I am excited about her work because she reflects me; she tells my story in a way and with an eloquence that is beyond my ability. She is sister and mother, lovingly fair; her anger controlled, her tears not quite hidden. She knows that mothers must eventually let sons and daughters stand on their own; she also knows that the tradition and politics of the West conspire to cut those sons and daughters down before they are able to magnify their lives:

> those boys that ran together
> at Tillman's
> and the poolroom
> everybody see them now
> think it's a shame
> everybody sec them now
> remember they was fine boys
>
> we have some fine Black boys,
> don't it make you want to cry? [C.T., p. 14]

Her tears are not maudlin, however: she strides, face wet with a fierce and angry water. And she keeps getting up from being down, keeps stealing future space. She is the woman of "long memory" coming from a long line "of Black and going women / who got used to making it through murdered sons." Clifton is an encourager, a pusher of the sons and daughters; a loving reminder of what was, is, must be.

She brings a Black woman's sensitivity to her poetry, brings the history of what it means to be a Black woman in America, and what she brings is not antagonistic, not stacked against Black men. When she speaks of the true enemy, it is done in a way that reinforces her humanity, yet displays a unique ability to capture the underlying reasons Europe wars on the world. Speaking of the "poor animal" and the "ape herds" of Europe, she says of them:

> he heads, always, for a cave
> his mind shivers against the rocks
> afraid of the dark afraid of the cold afraid to be alone
>
> afraid of the legendary man creature who is black

221

and walks on grass
and has no need for fire . . . [*C.T.*, p. 15]

For the Buffalo soldiers and for the Dahomey women, the two images that Bow throughout the body of much of her work, she sees a bright and difficult future. And she knows how to hurt, and she knows how to heal:

me and you be sisters
we be the same.
me and you
coming from the same place.
me and you
be greasing our legs ...
got babies
got thirty-five
got black ...
be loving ourselves
be sisters
only where you sing
i poet. [*A.O.W.*, p. 5]

Indeed, she poets. An understatement, she is like quality music; her works make you feel and care. She is also a folk historian, dealing not in dates and names but concepts. She is the original root woman, a connector to trees, earth, and the undestroyables, as in "On the Birth of Bomani":

We have taken the best leaves
and the best roots
and your mama whose skin
is the color of the sun
has opened into a fire and
your daddy whose skin
is the color of the night
has tended it carefully with
his hunter's hands and
here you have come, Bomani,
an African Treasure-Man.
may the art in the love that made you

fill your fingers,
may the love in the art that made you
your heart. [*A.O.W.*, p. 9]

Clifton's style is simple and solid, like rock and granite. She is a linear poet who uses very little of the page, an effective device for the free and open verse that she constructs. She is not an experimental poet. She has fashioned an uncomplicated and direct format that allows great latitude for incorporating her message.

She writes controlled and deliberate lines moving from idea to idea, image to image, building toward specific political and social concepts. She is at her best when she is succinct and direct:

love rejected
hurts so much more than Love rejecting;
they act like they don't love their country
No
what it is
is they found
their country don't love them. [*G.T.*, p. 23]

To conclude, Europeans put up statues for their dead poets or buy their homes and make them into museums. Often, they force their poets into suicide or nonproduction. Neglect for any writer is bitter, bitter salt, and Lucille Clifton's work has not seemed to take root in the adult segments of the Black reading community. Is it because she does not live in New York, may not have "connections" with reviewers nor possess Madison Avenue visibility? Is it that she needs more than a "mere" three books of poetry and a memoir? Is it that the major body of her work is directed toward children? Is it that her expressed moral and social values are archaic? All these possibilities are significant because they speak to the exchange nature of the game played daily in the publishing world; the only business more ruthless and corrupted is the Congress.

Clifton without doubt or pause is a Black woman (in color, culture, and consciousness); a family woman whose husband, children, and extended family have represented and played roles of great importance in her life and work, and a superb writer who will not compromise. She is considered among some to be a *literary find*; she is widely published and talked about, but, like most Black women writers, not promoted, and again, like most, her work can often be found in remainder bins less than a year after publication. (I bought fifty copies of *Generations* from a used book store.) Finally, she is serious about revolutionary change. Most writers that "make it" in this country have to become literary and physical prostitutes in one form or another. Clifton's work suggests that if she is to sell herself, it will be for benefits far greater than those which accrue from publishing a book. In recent Black literature, she is in the tradition of Gwendolyn Brooks, Mari Evans, and Sonia Sanchez. She will not compromise our people, is not to be played with, is loved and lover ("... you are the one I am lit for/come with your rod that twists and is a serpent/I am the bush/I am burning/I am not consumed"), is revolutionary, is, all beauty and finality, a Black woman:

> Lucille
> she calls the light, which was the name of the grandmother
> who waited by the crossroads
> in Virginia
> and shot the White man off his horse,
> killing the killer of sons.
> light breaks from her life
> to her lives . . .
> mine already is
> an Afrikan name. [*A.O.W.*, p. 73]

When we begin to rightfully honor the poets, Clifton will undoubtedly be gathering roses in her own community and miss the call. She is like that, a quiet unassuming person, yet bone-strong with vision of intense magnitude. She is new bone molded in African earth tested in West waters, ready for action:

> Other people think they know
> how long life is
> how strong life is/we know. [*A.O.W.*, p. 17]

To be original, relevant, and revolutionary in the mouth of fire is the mark of a dangerous person. Lucille Clifton is a poet of mean talent who has not let her gifts separate her from the work at hand. She is a teacher and an example. To read her is to give birth to bright seasons.

NOTES

1. Lucille Clifton, *An Ordinary Woman* (New York: Random House, 1974) p. 91. Hereafter referred to in text as *A.O.W.*
2. Lucille Clifton, *Good Times* (New York: Vintage Books 1970) p.1. Hereafter referred to in text as *G.T.*
3. Addison Gayle, Jr., *The War of the New World* (Garden City, N.Y.: Anchor Press/Doubleday, 1976), p. 307.

SONIA SANCHEZ: The Bringer of Memories

There are few writers alive who have created a body of work that both teaches and celebrates life, even at its darkest moments. Sonia Sanchez does this and more throughout her many volumes of poetry, short stories, plays, and children's books. She is prolific and sharp-eyed. Her telescopic view of the world is seldom light, frivolous or fraudulent. She is serious, serious to the point of pain and redemption. Her bottom line is this: she wants Black people to grow and develop so that we can move toward determining our own destiny. She wants us not only to be responsible for our actions but to take responsible actions. This is the task she has set for herself, and indeed she believes that what she can do others can do.

Her work is magic. Her scope and more often than not, her analytical mind, bring clarity and simplicity to the complicated. The brevity in her poetry has become her trademark:

> if i had known, if
> i had known you, i would have
> left my love at home.

She is a poet (and woman) of few but strong and decisive words. Her vision may sometime be controversial; nevertheless, it is her vision. With a sharing heart and mind, she is constantly seeking the perfect, always striving with an enduring passion toward an unattainable completeness.

Sanchez is best known for her poetry to which I will confine my remarks, but she is also a first-rate playwright and an accomplished children's writer and she has made a serious contribution to short fiction. She has written essays, but few have been published. Sanchez, not as well-known as Toni Morrison, Ntozake Shange, Alice Walker or Nikki Giovanni, has outproduced each of them and has been active in her chosen craft longer. The major reason she does not have the national celebrity her work and seriousness demand is that she does not compromise her values, her art, or her people for fame or gold. She is, undeniably the revolutionary whose sole aim is liberation, peace, love and effective writing.

Sanchez is specific; she is maximally concerned about the well-being her people, and much of her work relates this concern. She is not wide-eyed or romantic. The raising of her children, maintaining a home, working fourteen-hour days, doing serious cultural and political work, while creating an enduring body of poetry, has not allowed for too many misconceptions of the world. However, this is not to suggest that she not smile, love, or do things that make people whole and complicated. The point is that Sanchez is, as Toni Cade Bambara would state it: a "cultural worker" of the clearest and most accomplished rank.

Sanchez writes poetry that is forever questioning Black people's commitment to struggle. Much of her work intimately surveys the struggles between Black people and Black people, between Black and whites, between men and women, between self and self, and between cultures. She is always demanding answers, questioning motives and manners, looking for the complete story and not the easy surface that most of us settle for. Her poetry cuts to the main arteries of her people, sometimes drawing blood, but always looking for a way to increase the heartbeat and lower the blood pressure. Her poetry, for the most part, is therapeutic and cleansing. Much of her work is autobiographical, but not in the limiting sense that it is only about Sonia Sanchez. She is beyond the problem of a consuming ego, and with her, unlike many autobiographical writers, we are not always aware of the protagonist's actual identity. Black experiences in America are so similar and the normal distinctions that set Black people apart are not always obvious to outsiders. This is to note that, for the most part, her experiences are ours and vice versa. She is an optimistic realist searching the alleys for beauty as well as substance.

As a Black woman writer who is political, she brings a critical quality to her work that can easily overpower the nonpolitical reader. She is a lover, but her love is conditional, reflective, and selective. She is not given to an emotional romanticism of her people. This is not to suggest that she is not fresh or spontaneous in her reflections, but to acknowledge that she has indeed experienced life at its roller-coaster fullest from Cuba to China, from New York City to San Francisco to the confusion and strength of the international Black world. Sanchez is not, in terms of mind-set or communication, a tea leaf reader or stargazer. She has the major poet's quality; she is a visionary, unafraid to implant the vision.

Sonia Sanchez respects the power of Black language. More than any other poet, she has been responsible for legitimatizing the use of urban Black English in written form. Her use of language is spontaneous and thoughtful. Unlike many poets of the sixties, her use of the so-called profane has been innovatively shocking and uncommonly apropos. Her language is culturally legitimate and genuinely recollects the hard bottom and complicated spectrum of the entire Black community. She has taken Black speech and put it in the context of world literature.

This aspect of her world has often been overlooked. However, she, along with Baraka, Neal, Dumas and a few others of the sixties poets, must be looked upon as recorders and originators of an urban Black working language. Long before the discovery of Ntozake Shange, Sanchez set the tone and spaces of modern urban written Black poetry. In her early works, we can read and feel the rough city voices screaming full circle in all kinds of human settings as in "To Blk/Record/Buyers":

don't play me no
righteous bros.
white people
ain't rt bout nothing
no mo.
don't tell me, bout
foreign dudes
cuz no blk/
people are grooving on a
sunday afternoon.
they either
making out/
     signifying/
        drinking/
making molotov cocktails/
       stealing
or rather more taking their goods
from the honky thieves who
ain't hung up
     on no pacifist/jesus/
       cross   but
play blk/songs
          to drown out the
shit/screams of honkies. AAAH.
AAAH.   AAAH. yeah.   brothers.
   andmanymoretogo.

Language is one of the major tools used in the intellectual development of all people. The English language as the vehicle for communication in the United States varies from culture to culture. Part of the difficulty in communication between Blacks and whites is that whites do not listen to or respect serious communication from Blacks, and that whites do not understand, or prefer to ignore voices of the majority of Blacks. Whatever the reason, Sanchez understands them, and speaks, most forcefully and quite eloquently for herself, which is a creditable reflection of her community. Despite having located in academe (she is a tenured professor at Temple University), she has not separated herself from the roots of her people, and in most of her work we experience the urgency of Black life and a call for Black redemption and development.

She has effectively taken Black speech patterns, combined them with the internal music of her people, and injected progressive thoughts into her poetry. The best of the sixties poets always went past mere translation of the streets to transformation. Sanchez is a poet of enormous vision, and in each succeeding book one can view that vision deepening and broadening. She remains an intense and meticulous poet who has not compromised craft or skill for message. The content, the politics, are more effective because her language and style has enabled her to dissect the world in a fresh and meaningful manner.

BRINGER OF MEMORIES

All of Sanchez's books are significant *Homecoming* (1969) for its pace-setting language, *We a BadddDDD People* (1970) for its scope and maturity. Sanchez displays an uncommon ability for combining words and music, content and approach. The longer poems are work songs, and she continues to be devastating in the shorter works. *Love Poems* (1973), a book of laughter and hurt, smiles and missed moments, contains poems that expose the inner sides of Sanchez during the years 1964-73, in which she produces several masterworks. *A Blues Book for Blue Black Magical Women* (1974), her Black woman book, is a volume of sad songs and majestic histories. Her work becomes longer and ballad-like. This book highlights Black women as mothers, sisters, lovers, wives, workers, and warriors, an uncompromising commitment to the Black family, and the Black woman's role in building a better world. *I've Been a Woman: New and Select Poems* (1978) contains more than a decade of important work; it is truly an earth-cracking contribution. This book not only displays the staying power of Sonia Sanchez, but it also confirms her place among the giants of world literature. Throughout the entire body of her work, never apologizing, she affirms and builds a magnificent case for the reality of being Black and female, lashing out at all forms of racism, sexism, classism, just plain ignorance and stupidity. It must be noted that she was taking these positions before it was popular and profitable.

A bringer of memories, Sanchez gives us just short of two decades of poetry which emphasizes struggle and history in poetic pictures; photographs, in which she as writer and participant was intimately involved. She does not let us forget. Her work is a reminder of what was and is. She has experienced two lifetimes. Her poetic range is impressive and enlightening as she comments on subjects as diverse as Black studies and the Nation of Islam—from Malcolm X to Sterling Brown, unmistakably showing us that she is both player and observer in this world.

If you wish to measure the strength of a people, examine its culture. The cultural forces more than any other connector are the vehicles that transmit values from one generation to another. In studying Sanchez's poetry, we see a person immersed in her people's history, religion, politics, social structure, ethics and psychology. She is forever pushing for Black continuation, as in "For Unborn Malcolms," where she urges Black retaliation for white violence:

> its time
> an eye for an eye
> a tooth for a tooth
> don't worry bout his balls
>
> they al
> ready gone.
> git the word
> out that us blk/niggers
> are out to lunch
> and the main course
> is gonna be his white meat.
> yeah.

As a cultural poet, Sonia Sanchez is uniquely aware of the complexity and confusion of her people. She translates this world effectively, yet somehow even in her most down times, she projects richness and lively tomorrows. In the best of her work she is establishing tradition.

It would be condescending to state that she is original. She is so original she had difficulty getting published in the early days; her beauty and compactness of words are sometimes matched only by Carol Freeman and Norman Jordan. Nevertheless, although the major small journals that published Black poets exclusively and introduced the poets to each other and the community (*Journal of Black Poetry, Soul Book, Liberator and Negro Digest/Black World*) frequently provided a national outlet for Sanchez as well as other poets of her generation.

Dudley Randall's Broadside Press was responsible for publishing Sonia Sanchez's early books as well as those of a good many of the sixties poets. Sanchez delivers many aspects of Black life with a sharpness, a precision, that closely resembles rapping and signifying. In less skilled hands, this would not have worked, but Sanchez's strength has been to take the ordinary and make it art, make it memorable. The multiple sides of the poet were first demonstrated in her book *We a BaddDDD People* (1970), where she carefully and lovingly surveyed the Black world. The first selection, "Survival Poems," is a mirror of our years. She comments on everything from suicide to her relationship to poet Etheridge Knight to whom she was married at the time. If there are any problems with *We a BaddDDD People* it may be with form. In a few of the poems, i.e., "A Chant for Young/Brothas and Sistuhs" she is too easy with the message; she does not force the reader to work or to reflect. The effectiveness of her use of slashes to separate words and lines is questionable.

    seen yo/high
        on every blk/st in
    wite/amurica
        i've seen yo/sell/
    imposed/quarantined/hipness
        on every
    slum/bar/
        revolutionary/st

However, the form does work when the message doesn't overpower the style. Her poem "There Are Blk/Puritans" is an excellent example of irony and substance. She argues for a new and developed political awareness, demanding that her readers locate the actual profanity in their lives:

    there are blk/puritans
    among us
        straight off the
    mayflower
        who wud have u
    believe
        that the word
    fuck/u/mutha/fucka
          is evil

                    un/black.
               who wud
     ignore the real/curse/words
     of our time
               like.   CA/PITA/LISM
     blk/pimps
               nixonandco
          COMMUNISM.
     missanne
               rocke/FELLER
                    there
     are blk/puritans among us
     who must be told that
     WITE/AMURICA
                    is the
     only original sin.

Immediately noticeable in this poem are (1) a sense of history--getting off the *Mayflower,* means Black people came from somewhere else—and suggests a polarity, an intragroup dichotomy; (2) questioning values--the system of exploiting capitalism vs. curse words, i.e., which is the real evil; (3) the use of Black language: blk, wud, mutha, fucka, wite, Amurica; (4) the negative effects of acculturation, blk/puritans/among us; and (5) an identification of the undeniable evils of this world: "CA/PITA/LISM, blk/ pimps, nixonandco, COMMUNISM, missanne, rocke/FELLER and WITE/AMURICA." The spelling of America as AMURICA is to denote the murdering quality of this land, which, as she sees it, is the "original sin."

Throughout this section of *We A BaddDDD People*, Sanchez is concerned with Black-on-Black damage, especially in the area of social relationships, i.e., family:

     and i mean.
               like if brothas
     programmed sistuhs to love
     instead of
                    fucken/hood
                         and i mean
     if mothas prognmmed

                    sistuhs to
good feelings bout they blk/men
and i
        mean if blk/fathas proved
they man/hood by
                    fighten the enemy
instead of fucken every available sistuh
and i mean
                if we programmed/loved/each
other in com/mun/al ways
                    so that no
blk/person starved
            or killed
                    each other on
a sat/ur/day nite corner.
then may
            be   it wud all
come down to some
                    thing else
like RE VO LU TION.
                i mean if
                    like yeh.

It is interesting that in later books, especially *Love Poems*, and I've Been a Wom-
an, she forsakes syllable separation and overuse of page and concentrates
more on the fresh juxtaposition of words within context. The overuse of the
page and the seemingly confusing punctuation prevalent in *Homecoming* and
We a BaddDDD People all but disappear in later poetry and are not highlighted
in her selected poems.

      Sanchez has always been the sharpest in locating the tragedies in our lives
and she is not one to bite her tongue or forge false messages. She goes directly
to the bone. Like a skilled chiropractor, she locates the spine and carefully and
professionally makes the correct adjustments. In "Present," from *A Blues Book
for Blue Black Magical Women:*

there is no place
for a soft/black/woman.
there is no smile green enough or
summertime words warm enough to allow my growth.
and in my head
i see my history
standing like a shy child
and i chant lullabies
as i ride my past on horseback
tasting the thirst of yesterday tribes
hearing the ancient/black/woman
me, singing   hay-hay-hay-hay-ya-ya-ya.
                     hay-hay-hay-hay-ya-ya-ya.

like a slow scent
beneath the sun . . .

She is always seeking fulfillment—bridging generations looking for answers, forever disturbing the dust in our acculturated lives. Her work represents cultural stabilizers at their best. As Geneva Smitherman noted in her book *Talkin and Testifyin: The Language of Black America*:

What the new black poets have done, then, is to take. for their conceptual and expressive tools a language firmly rooted in the black experience. Such terms and expressions enable the poets to use cultural images and messages familiar to their black audiences, and with great strokes of brevity, Black English lines and phrases reveal a complete story. (Such, of course, is the way any good poet operates; what a unique here is the effective execution of the operation in a black way.)

Much of Sanchez's poetry is painful and challenging; *that she continues to love the miracle.* How can a Black man not be touched and moved by poems such as "For Unborn Malcolms" and "Past"? In the earlier work, there seemed to be little peace within her, and the forces that were tearing her apart ripped at our souls also. However, Sanchez cannot be boxed into any single category even though most of her work deals with some aspect of Black redemption. The book that represents this multifaceted characteristic, in addition to displaying other sides of the poet's nature is *Love Poems* (1973).

Love Poems is a startling and profound departure from Sanchez's other books. It's introspective and meditative. The poems are highly personal and complex. For the untried reader, some of the poems will require three and four readings. The book is less experimental, and she has basically made use of traditional poetic forms such as haiku and ballad. The poetry is delicate, rich, and very honest. There are illustrations to complement the poetry, and between the line drawings and poems, there is an air of quiet patience created.

Love Poems represents close to a decade of sunsets, hangovers, and the woman, as poet, ignites and brings forth fire in this book, and most appropriately, food. She continues this voice in *A Blues Book for Blue Black Magical Women,* yet in Love Poems there is a great tenderness, a willingness to touch the reader. She is seeking distilled communication, clearing paths so that nothing separates the poet from the reader. She succeeds beautifully; there are few obstacles; her form is relaxed, the lines easy, flowing. Her language has appropriate colorations and the content is tri-dimensional: (1) an unusual, yet effective openness, (2) razor sharp brevity that painlessly cuts into the heart, and (3) a womanly seriousness—strong and unmoving—like trying to remove black from coal, an impossible task unless you destroy or burn the coal.

The titles of the poems are not descriptive; instead they are convenient identifiers in "July":

> the old men and women
> quilt their legs
> in the shade
> while tapestry pigeons
> strut their necks.
> as i walk, thinking
> about you my love,
> i wonder what it is
> to be old
> and swallow death each day
> like warm beer.

One can see a marriage beginning to break as she talks to us in Poem No. 2:

> my puertorican
> husband who feeds me
> cares for me and loves me

        is trying to under
stand my Blackness.
so he is taking up
watercolors.

Much of the poetry is about the men in her life, and one immediately notices the change in attitude toward her father. From the poem "A Poem for My Father" of *We a BaddDDD People* to the two-part poem "Father and Daughter" of Love Poems there is an escalation of understanding that belies her young years. The earlier poem speaks of "perfumed bodies weeping / underneath you," and "when i remember your deformity I want to / do something about your / makeshift manhood. I guess that is why / on meeting your sixth / wife I cross myself with her confessions." This poem is cold and unforgiving and seems to lack understanding. "Father and Daughter" of *Love Poems* (there is also another "Father and Daughter" in *I've Been a Woman*) is a compelling and unforgettable reading of emotions from the daughter, who states in Part One, "It is difficult to believe that we / even talked. How did we spend the night while seasons passed in place of words." However, the complexity of the love the poet feels for her father as well as the distance between them, and a newfound understanding, is inescapable in Part Two:

        you cannot live hear and bend my heart
        amid the rhythm of your screams. Apart
        still venom sleeps and drains down thru the years
        touch not these hands once live with shears
        i live a dream about you; each man
        alone. You need the sterile wood old age can
        bring, no opening of the veins whose smell
        will bruise light bread and burst our shell
        of seeds, the landslide of your season
        burns the air: this mating has no reason.
        don't cry, late grief is not enough. the motion
        of your tides still flows within; the ocean
        of deep blood that downs the land. we die:
        while young moons rage and wander in the sky.

The men in Sanchez's life have brought both joy and hurt and the experi-ence is without a doubt a common thread that connects Black women to each other as well as their men. All Black women have been influenced by Black men—be they their fathers, brothers, lovers, husbands, sons, or friends; they affect the women in a multitude of ways both negative and positive, such as:

> Now. i at
> thirty. You at
> thirty-two are
> sculptured stains
> and my death
> comes with
> enormous eyes
> and my dreams
> turn in deformity.

and the positive is thought-provoking:

> and what of the old bearded man collecting
> bottles who pulls a burlap bag behind?
> if we speak of love,
> what of his black body arched over the city
> opening the scales of strangers
> carrying the dirt of corners to his hunched corner?
> if we know of love
> we rest;
> while the world moves wrenched by collection.

Love Poems was published during the period that Sanchez was a member of the Nation of Islam, and during those years the unofficial position of the NOI was to read little other than the recommended text. It is remarkable that there are only a few references in *Love Poems* that remind us of her religious conversion. One of the powerful things about the collection is that it defies ideological positioning, and the other quality is that the poems indicate that she seems to be at peace with herself. This peacefulness comes across in several memorable poems:

> there are things sadder
> than you and I, some people
> do not even touch.

There are two masterworks, "To All brothers: From All Sisters" and "Old Worlds." The first and final stanzas of "Old Words" follow:

> we are the dead
> ones the slow
> fast suicides of our time.
> we are the dis
> enfranchised ones
> the buyers of bread
> one day removed
> from mold
> we are maimed
> in our posture...
>
> we have to come to
> believe that we are
> not. to be we
> must be loved or
> touched and proved
> to be. this earth
> turns old
> and rivers grow lunatic
> with rain. how I wish
> I could lean in your cave
> and creak with the winds.

This book is almost too beautiful—a somewhat sad beauty containing lines and stanzas that other poets wish that they had written. In Love Poems, Sanchez is more lyrical in a subtle way. Her descriptive powers are full-blown; she is quietly dramatic, yet her slices of life re never soap operaish or exploitative as in this haiku:

> we grow up my love
> because as yet there is no
> other place to go

The book *I've Been a Woman: Selected and New Poems flows,* is river-like and thirst quenching. It is a poet's book containing landscapes and mountains with few valleys. This collection is the history of Sanchez as poet—a poet consistently at her best, spanning the entire range of her talent. A carefully selected volume, it is a clear indication of the growth and genius of the poet. Selected poems, unlike a poet's collected poems, is not a life's work. It is more midlife, a middle years' comment of the poet as well as statements that suggest or indicate what is to come.

The two poems for Sterling Brown are a warm and glowing tribute from one poet to another:

> I'm gonna get me some mummy tape for love
> preserve it for 3000 years or more
> I'm gonna let the world see you
> tapping a blue shell dance of love

In this collection she includes another "Father and Daughter" that rocks with color and intimate observations. It seems that her father will continue to be a subject of much discussion in future works. However, the poem that will undoubtedly live for ages is "Kwa Mamu Zetu Waliotuzaa" (For Our Mother Who Gave Birth). This work, the last piece in the collection, is a stunning three-part epic calling mothers (a special final tribute to Shirley Graham Dubois) to recapture sunlight and peace while acknowledging . . .

> death is a five o'clock door forever changing time.
>   and it was morning without sun or shadow;
> a morning already afternoon. sky. cloudy with incense.
>   and it was morning male in speech;
> feminine in memory.
> But i am speaking of everyday occurrences:
> of days unrolling bandages for civilized wounds;
> of gaudy women chanting rituals under a waterfall of stars;
> of men freezing theirs sperms in diamond-studded wombs;
> of children abandoned to a curfew of marble.

Yet, for the poet, "at the Center of death is birth" represents the real focus of her poetry. She is hungry for life. Trapped in America, she like us has had to make small compromises in position—not values—such as having race and economics determining where we live and work. As a seeker of truth, as a pathfinder in the area of communicative writing, Sanchez has few peers. She falls beautifully in the tradition of Gwendolyn Brooks, Margaret Walker, Langston Hughes, Zora Neale Hurston, Sterling Brown, and Shirley Graham Dubois.

She has few peers that can match the urgency, anger and love found in her work. There are few who can look over two decades of work and feel good and pleased for taking the long, difficult road and coming out scared, but not cut, not devoid of future:

> i am circling new boundaries
> i have been trailing the ornamental
> songs of death (life
> a strong pine tree
> dancing in the wind
> i inhale the ancient black breath
> cry for every dying (living
> creature
>
> come. let us ascend from the
> middle of our breath
> sacred rhythms
> inhaling peace.

Sanchez has been an inspiration to a generation of young poets. In my travels, she, Mari Evans, and Gwendolyn Brooks are the women writers most often admired. Her concreteness and consistency over those many years is noteworthy. She has not bought refuge from day-to-day struggles by becoming a writer of Western tradition. Her involvement in struggle has fueled her writing so that she is seldom boring or overly repetitious. Somehow, one feels deep inside that in a real fight this is the type of Black woman you would want at your side. In her work she brings clarity to the world and in so doing she, unlike many writers, transcends our conception of what a poet does.

There is no last word for a poet. Poets sign their own signatures on the world. Those who comment on their greatness do so only because greatness is often confused with the commonplace in this country. The singers of the new songs understand the world that is coming because they are the makers. This includes Sonia Sanchez.

Haki R. Madhubuti (formerly Don L. Lee) is currently director of the Institute of Positive Education and editor of Third World Press, Chicago. The author of eleven books of poetry, criticism, and essays, he is a popular lecturer and the recipient of numerous, awards. His most recent publication in Earthquake and Sunrise Missions (1983), his first published poetry volume in a decade.

BAMBARA: What She Meant To Us/Me

"Men have got to develop some heart and some sound analysis
to realize that when sisters get passionate about themselves
and their direction, it does not mean they're readying up to kick
men's ass. They're readying up for honesty. And women have got
to develop some heart and some sound analysis so they can resist
the temptation of buying peace with their man with self-sacrifice
and posturing. The job then regarding "roles" is to submerge all
breezy definitions of manhood/womanhood (or reject them out
of hand if you're not squeamish about being called "neuter")
until realistic definitions emerge through a commitment to Blackhood."

—Toni Cade Bambara from "on the issue of Roles" from
The Black Woman ed. by Toni Cade

There is brilliance and bravery written here, among the cultures of masculinity and "men run it;" there is a clear message here for the youthful years and innocent eyes of "I'll make us a world" students. Toni Cade in her critical, original and singular anthology *The Black Woman* (1970) opened the door for serious dialogue among young men like myself who were deeply involved in street struggle, writing, teaching, on-going study, institution building and interaction and loving Black women. I was raised in a male-centered and racist culture, be it Black (negro at that time) operating subservient to the Euro-male politics of white supremacy and white world nationalism. My early readings of W.E.B. DuBois, Malcolm X, Frantz Fanon, Richard Wright, Carter G. Woodson and others informed (initiated) me and millions of others to this reality.

However, it was Toni Cade, before becoming Bambara along with Margaret Burroughs, Barbara Ann Sizemore, Gwendolyn Brooks, Ella Baker, Fannie Lou Hamer, Rosa Parks, Sonia Sanchez and hundreds of local and national Black women in struggle and cultural work who gently slapped me and other men into a new consciousness, into what sister Toni defined as "Blackhood." Truth be told, it started much earlier for me. My mother worked in the sex trade and the weekly struggles she endured to love, feed, house and educate me and my sister were insurmountable and drove her to drugs, alcohol and dangerous communities resulting in her "untimely" death at the age of thirty-four. Therefore, my life circumstances forced me to – at a very young age – to assess the lives of women differently than most Black boys and men.

Unconsciously, around the age of fourteen I began to study and sought out "strong" women and men to mentor me. These mentorships drove me to Black literature and when *The Black Woman* was published in 1970, I immediately read and studied its content which confirmed my own understanding of Black struggle and relationships, especially this passage by Toni Cade:

> Revolution begins with the self, in the self. The individual, the basic revolutionary unit, must be purged of poison and lies that assault the ego and threaten the heart, that hazard the next larger unit—the family or cell, that put the entire movement in peril. We make many false starts because we have been programmed to depend on white models or white interpretations of non-white models, so we don't even ask the correct questions, much less begin to move in a correct direction. Perhaps we need to face the terrifying and overwhelming possibility that there are no models, that we shall have to create from scratch. Doctrinaire Marxism is basically incompatible with Black nationalism; New Left politics is incompatible with Black nationalism; doctrinaire socialism is incompatible with Black revolution; capitalism, lord knows, is out. We need to reject too the opinions of outside "experts" who love to explain ourselves to ourselves, telling the Black man that the matriarch is his enemy.

We artist, including Ms. Cade were in the middle of the Black Arts Movement (BAM). Black artist of all disciplines were actively re-defining, exploring, working, acting-out, meeting, covering conferences and conventions, building Black independent institutions such as schools, bookstores, magazines, newspapers and workers co-ops and unions. We had, along with Third World Press and our schools, two Black bookstores and when in October of 1972 a book titled *Gorilla, My Love* by Toni Cade Bambara hit our shelves, I read it in two sittings and began to share and teach it at Howard University where I was on faculty at that time. I did not realize that Toni Cade had changed her name. However, a few of the BAM artist in their quest to redefine themselves and their worlds changed their names, LeRoi Jones became Amiri Baraka and I, Don L. Lee became Haki R. Madhubuti. Rediscovering Toni Cade Bambara, as a fiction writer of immense talent, insight and moral and ethnic grounding was a joy. In this collection, I realized that I was among greatness when I read her short story "The Lesson." As a poet, I am unusually tuned to language, what's said and what is not said, the local scripture of word usage, one's choices, articulations and combinations. I knew that I was hung up on reading this from the first paragraph of "The Lesson":

> Back in the days when everyone was old and stupid or young and foolish and me and Sugar were the only ones just right, this lady moved on our block with nappy hair and proper speech and no makeup. And quite naturally we laughed at her, laughed the way we did at the junk man who went about his business like he was some big-time president and his sorry-ass horse his secretary. And we kinda hated her too, hated the way we did the winos who cluttered up our parks and pissed on our handball walls and stank up our hallways and stairs so you couldn't halfway play hide-and-seek without a goddamn gas mask. Miss Moore was her name. The only woman on the block with no first name. And she was always planning these boring-ass things for us to do, us being my cousin, mostly, who lived on the block cause we all moved North the same time and to the same apartment then spread out gradual to breathe. And our parents would yank our heads into some kinda shape and crisp up our clothes so we'd be presentable for travel with Miss Moore, who always looked like she was going to church, though she never did.

During the years of BAM (1965-1976), I traveled almost weekly across the nation and internationally. In 1974, after the publication of my latest book of poems *Book of Life,* I was invited to Spelman College. After my reading that evening I was informed that Toni Cade Bambara was teaching there. The next day I, uninvited, walked into her class and was greeted by her with a large, all teeth showing smile and applause from the twenty or so students. This was our first meeting but not the last.

As a poet who has been cultural, highly political, often revolutionary in thoughts and actions I knew upon meeting and talking to sista Bambara that I had met a kindred spirit, a sister of her <u>word</u>, and a writer soon to be film maker – who would continue to impact the nation and world with her work. I also know that just as I, she would agree with Adrienne Rich in this statement from "Poetry and Commitment":

> "I'm both a poet and one of the "every bodies" of my country. I live, in poetry and daily experience, with manipulated fear, ignorance, cultural confusion, and social antagonism huddling together on the fault line of an empire. In my lifetime I've seen the breakdown of rights and citizenship where ordinary "every bodies," poets or not, have left politics to a political class bent on shoveling the elemental resources, the public commons of the entire world into

private control. Where democracy has been left to the raiding of "acknowledged" legislators, the highest bidders. In short, to a criminal element.

Where Ms. Rich used the word "poet" let us replace her words with "artist" and her statement becomes more inclusive for all including Ms. Bambara. Let me end with deep appreciation and love from her own sisterhood. Yes, I am a part of Bambara's "Blackhood" and a loving brother to the bone. However, if I've learned anything in struggle, I absorbed and acknowledged the code of sisters. Her relationship to Toni Morrison was as if they came from the same mother. There were many, many others; two who were special were Sonia Sanchez and Dr. Eleanor W. Traylor. In talking to Professor Sanchez she quoted Toni Cade Bambara:

> "Once you understand what your work is and you do not try to avert your eyes from it, but attempt to invest energy in getting that work done, the universe will send you what you need. You simply have to know how to be still and receive it."

and Professor Sanchez continues to enlighten:

> Indeed, that's what our dear sister Toni Cade Bambara did as she documented our bones. She. Black woman. Mother. She. World traveler. Community organizer. She practicing saint of hands threading our lives with beauty and hope. And spirit. She. Dawn mother. Born in song and prayer.... singing words of life...life...life. She genius woman.

Dr. Traylor mines the field of other writers to add to her own love-note:

> The pride and joy of Toni resides somewhere amid Amiri's embodiment of her as spirit of "our bright revolutionary generation. And its fantastic desires. Its beauty. Its strength. Its struggles. Its accomplishments." For Valerie Boyd, "she was just outrageously brilliant." Pearl Cleage calls her "sister writer, cultural worker, mother extraordinaire, and loyal friend." For Avery Gordon, she compels "something more powerful than skepticism." For Cheryl A. Wall, she is "a musical obbligato, an indispensable voice, an essential component of the composite of its era." For Toni Morrison, "she was one of our finest writers." And for me, something wonderful pervades the universe of Toni Cade Bambara, something like "new possibilities forever in formation" to "save the planet from the psychopath."

One of our last meetings was in 1986 (see enclosed photo by the poet Lamont Brown Steptoe) at a conference in Philadelphia organized by Dr. Eleanor W. Traylor. For me she remains the unique questioner among us, seeking the uncommon, sub-surface entrance into the book of knowledge. The smiling sister reflecting a quiet quality directing us with her many whys, *are you sure looks. Let's go at this from another angle.* She was the "cultural worker" always grounding us, always leading by example toward that which was good, just, correct and right. It was her carved in imagination and struggle. Toni Morrison, in her book *Playing in the Dark,* comments rather emphatically on the abuse and distortions of Black folk in western literature:

> My early assumptions as a reader were that black people signified little or nothing in the imagination of white American writers. Other than as the objects of an occasional bout of jungle fever, other than to provide local color or to lend some touch of verisimilitude or to supply a needed moral gesture, humor, or bit of pathos, blacks made no appearance at all.

Toni Cade Bambara and the poets, writers, musicians, film makers, actors, playwrights, visual artist, dancers, institution builders, educators and others of the Black Arts Movement helped to change this racist version of Black people to one that is more complete and complicated, intricate and human. She states it best in the dedication of *The Black Woman:*

> The book is dedicated to the uptown mammas who nudged me to just set it down in print so it gets to be a habit to write letters to each other, so maybe that way we don't keep tread milling the same old ground.

Well, count me in and contemplate on what we are missing without our dear sister and cultural worker. Statistically and emotionally, her value cannot be codified. She knew and her life's work expresses, that the best way to effectively fight an alien culture is to live your own.

REMEMBERING MAYA ANGELOU

We have just lost another mountain, one that has never been scaled or fully surveyed. Maya at 86 was a poet, author, autobiographer, playwright, civil rights worker, African liberation activist, professor, teacher and an accomplished singer, actor and dancer.

She was indeed a multitalented woman who took on the world at a time when the world needed her message. It's widely known that when she was young, while living in St. Louis, Maya was raped by her mother's boyfriend. She confided in her brother, who informed the rest of the family, and the man, whom Maya identified as "Mr. Freeman," was found guilty but spent only one day in jail. Soon after he was released, Freeman was mysteriously murdered. As a result of this trauma, Maya became mute for almost five years, believing that Freeman was killed because she told his name and therefore thought that she would never speak again thinking that her voice could kill.

During this profound period of silence, she developed a phenomenal memory and her love for literature, music and the rhymes of the black community grew. According to her autobiography, a Mrs. Bertha Flowers, a teacher and family friend, introduced her to the works of Dickens, Shakespeare, Poe, James Weldon Johnson and Georgia Douglas Johnson.

Fast forward to 1959 when she moved to New York at the encouragement of the great fiction writer John O. Killens (who would later be a strong influence in my own work). During this period Killens and writers such as Richard Wright, Chester Hines and Ralph Ellison were making their mark on Western literature. Poets Langston Hughes, Melvin B. Tolson, Robert Hayden, Margaret Walker and Gwendolyn Brooks were not far behind. Zora Neale Hurston was making her mark, and a young James Baldwin was tearing up the pages of national journals. Maya entered this company of writers and fell into the warm arms of the Harlem Writers Guild. There she met many of the writers who influenced me and thousands of others: Paule Marshall, Rosa Guy, Julian Mayfield and the historian John Henrik Clarke.

I first met Maya in the early 1970s through poet Eugene B. Redmond. During the period of the Black Arts Movement, we would encounter each other all over the nation. Redmond, the poet laureate of East St. Louis in 1976, became Maya's cultural brother for life. He told me Wednesday that whenever they met, they would do three things: 1) tell stories (lies), 2) take a drink and 3) enjoy home-cooked food. In his recent collection, *Arkansippi Memwars, Poetry, Prose & Chants,* Redmond writes:

Maya's cookin' tonight:
Proof's in metaphors we've plucked from tunnels & heights
to bake anthems & epics for familistic rites.
Under strobes & frennels made of stars & scars, we strutted
kitchen stages
with the mean & cream of soul cuisine.
Churing nouns into verbs, she said we'd
sister & brother each other.

In the 1990s, Maya was invited to Chicago State University, where I was teaching, to keynote the annual Gwendolyn Brooks Conference. We could not afford to pay her the full honorarium, but she, out of serious respect for Ms. Brooks, arrived in all of her smiles, wonderment and verse — showering all of us, including Ms. Brooks, with her magic. As she left that evening, she asked me to walk with her to her car and, despite walking hand in hand, she managed to slip into my pocket the honorarium that we had paid her. She demanded that it be donated to the university.

That is who she was.

In 2004, Howard University honored the poet with its
Maya Angelou Day, and I wrote the poem, "Maya: We Honor Our Own"
for the occasion, which is included in this collection

NTOZAKE SHANGE: Never Wrong-Eyed

i.

We poets know poets. We cannot, do not hide from each other. We read each other. Listen to each other with shared eyes and ears. Where others read, hear conflict or anger, we see, feel and hear love. We play with language: spelling, improbable but accurate word soundings, improvised human context, unusual uses of punctuation, street vernacular, the lingua franca of home, prisons, historically Black colleges and universities, Black male or female organizations (gangs), and for escaping negroes in the Ivy Leagues. Poets understand the disrupting often disquieting overwork that goes into creating and confront the great possibilities of being misunderstood.

Ntozake Shange changed the landscape for many of us. She, along with Zora Neale Hurston, Gwendolyn Brooks, Ruby Dee, Toni Cade Bambara, Toni Morrison, Audre Lorde, Maya Angelou, Sonia Sanchez, Alice Walker, Margaret Walker, Nikki Giovanni and others started a much needed healing in the Black community. One cannot read them and not be moved to think, contemplate and give up on the overused conventional stereotyped, and cliché written views of women, and Black women in particular. Their creative and political production not only aided Black men, but also impacted young Black women to critical points in their lives to which they now embody the most powerful force for good in the nation today. This is pre-*Black Girls Rock*.

Often, Black men, listened to and read Ntozake incorrectly. To be raised in, challenged, acculturated to and beaten down by white supremacist patriarchal culture oftentimes produced too many Black men who were and are still today traumatized and insensitive to many outside of their immediate and extended families. Yet, those women who are the closest—or as Ntozake so impactfully writes about—become affected the greatest, hurt the deepest, disrespected often beyond repair. In an insightful interview with Claudia Tate, editor of the wonderful book *Black Women Writers at Work* (1983) sister Shange states, "When you are living lies, you don't know what's real." Black poets and artists in general know that America is the greatest lie ever constructed among the family of nations. Its history in reference to native peoples, Africans, all Black and Brown people is beyond exploited, it is murderous. It is genocidal. Shange also states in the same interview:

The reason that *For Colored Girls* is entitled *For Colored Girls* is that's who it was for. I wanted them to have information that I did not have. I wanted them to know what it was truthfully like to be a grown woman. I didn't know. All I had was a bunch of mythology-tales and outright lies. I wanted a 12-year-old girl to reach out and get some information that isn't just contraceptive information but emotional information... but I don't want them to grow in a void of misogynist lies. If there is an audience for whom I write, it's the little girls who are coming of age. I want them to know that they are not alone and that we adult women thought and continue to think about them.

That she spoke to young girls is the highest and most profound statement of love. I have daughters, all strong, self-aware, self-conscious, culturally, politically and critically intelligent, self-determining and not fearful of Black men. Their emotional and cultural intelligence as well as many young women in the nation is partially due to the works of Zake, their mothers, aunties, fathers and others.

The advanced artist, Ntozake Shange was always on call to do battle with lies and ugliness wherever they originated. Yet, she was often alone as most artists are and in need of affirmation and emotional support herself. This personal observation is shared with us in a recent essay in The Nation (12-3-18) by Rebecca Carroll. Above all, artists of all stripes, creating in all fields, is a liberating and disruptive process, demanding every inch of one's psychic energy. How did Zake release and rejoin the natural flow of her human saneness? Her life especially after the success of For Colored Girls on Broadway was mildly stated—complicated.

Ntozake Shange was a "star." Singular in her many voices: chorepoet, playwright, novelist, essayist, actor, director, professor, teacher, arts activists, wife (two times), mother, friend, sister, and mentor to thousands. She was inherently cultural and political in a time of ultra white-whiteness. Her voice still radiates in her recently published *Wild Beauty: New and Selected Poems of Ntozake Shange* (2017), which includes a complete Spanish text. We have read poetry together several times over the years and we honored her in Chicago at one of our annual Gwendolyn Brooks Writer's Conferences. With game changing abilities, she was a Black library, anti-ignorance, authoritative and understood nuance and tragedy, love and occupation, always traveling quietly and loudly searching sub-surface for meanings and answers. In the interview with Claudia Tate she also reveals:

for me James Brown, Earth, Wind & Fire, the Art Ensemble of Chicago, Cecil Taylor, Pacheco and Rodriguez are all *high* art. I will stick to my guns about that. We do not have to refer continually to European art as the standard. That's absolutely absurd and racist, and I won't participate in that utter lie. My work is one of the few ways I can preserve the elements of our culture that need to be remembered and absolutely revered.

This, actually is also the anthem of most of the artists of the Black Arts Movement, quiet as its kept, she loved us.

ii.
never wrong-eyed, a period and a question,
ears always closed to the forgotten,
the beaten down/up clothesless, homeless,
under-loved, forever talked about
hands on hip women, always & always
searching for their freedom voices.
a warrior in the oral tradition with a graduate degree
and community theatre uniqueness and creds
find her in your heart, your front room of honesty:
bone Black, soul Black , quick overnight Black, no excuses Black, grandmama's greens Black,
adult reading room Black, toussaint l'overture Black, eight year old free Haiti Black,
memory & rememory Black, sixties/seventies black arts movement Black,
renaming Black Black, "idea that letters dance" Black, advanced conscious-ness
Black, "not blk enuf" Black, humanely honest Black, minstrel dance Black,
"roughness and the rawness" Black, "fatmama Black," long hand writer Black,
"smelldirt" Black, spanish english french portuguese Black, "mood indigo"
Black, "closed fists" Black, liveoak Black, "power to feed, nourish
& educate" Black, "crack annie" Black, bob marley Black,
"what love sounds like" Black, "new pussy" Black,
"comin to undo what's been done" Black.

Zake was a musician with language. She was a Black Arts visionary living long enough to see the ripe fruit, green vegetables, the legalization and acceptance of Black studies, and swim among the builders, rule makers of sisters and brothers that her words made. However, it is best to end in her words from Tate's interview:

> When I die, I will not be guilty of having left a generation of girls behind thinking that anyone can tend to their emotional health other than themselves. We see women who at fifty, look back at their lives; they are either very bitter or very childlike because their development was arrested. It is not incumbent upon us for this to happen as much as it is incumbent upon our mothers.

In *Wild Beauty: New and Selected Poems of Ntozake Shange,* we read the mature, highly indigenous, accomplished, overlearned, seasoned, full blossomed and now iconic ancestor Zake. It must also be noted that she created literature for boys, brothers, sons, fathers, uncles, grandfathers and all poets who love dancing with letters. She will remain our elephant in the room listening, listening and walking tall, helping all of us to form a nation of Black, Brown and others of us.

YOU WILL RECOGNIZE YOUR BROTHERS

You will recognize your brothers
by the way the act and move throughout the world.
there will be a strange force about them,
there will be unspoken answers in them.
this will be obvious not only to you to many.
the confidence they have in themselves and in
their people will be evident in their saneness.
the way they relate to women will be
clean, complimentary, responsible, with honesty and as partners.
the way they relate to children will be
strong and soft full of positive direction and as example.
the way they relate to men
will be that of questioning our position in this world,
will be one of planning for movement and change,
will be one of working for their people,
will be one of gaining and maintaining trust within the culture.
these men at first will seem strange and unusual but
this will not be the case for long.
they will train other and the discipline they display
will be a way for life for many.
they know that this is difficult
but this is the life that they have chosen
for themselves, for us, for life:
they will be the examples,
they will the answers, they will be the first line builders,
they will be the creators,
they will be the first to give up the weakening pleasures,
they will be the first to give up the weakening pleasures,
they will be the first to share a black value system
they will be the workers,
they will be the scholars,
they will be the providers,
they will be the historians,
they will be the doctors, lawyers, farmers, priests
and all that is needed for development and growth.
you will recognize these brother
and
they will not betray you.

for John Thompson

ABOUT THE AUTHOR

A leading poet and one of the architects of the Black Arts Movement, Haki R. Madhubuti, publisher, editor, educator and activist—has been a pivotal figure in the development of a strong Black literary tradition. His love for Black literature matured while serving in the US Army (1960-63) in between wars where the army's motto was "hurry up and wait"; he waited with books primarily from used bookstores which became a second home. His third book *Don't Cry Scream* with an introduction by Gwendolyn Brooks, sold over 75,000 copies during its first year of publication as a result of a feature article by David Llorens which appeared in the March 1969 issue of *Ebony* magazine. He has published more than 30 books – including 14 books of poetry - (some under his former name, Don L. Lee) and is one of the world's best-selling authors of poetry and nonfiction. Professor Madhubuti's *Black Men: Obsolete, Single, Dangerous? The African American Family in Transition* (1990) has over 1 million copies in print. Selected titles include: *From Plan to Planet: Life Studies, The Need for Afrikan Minds and Institutions* (1973); *Tough Notes: A Healing Call for Creating Exceptional Black Men* (2002); *Run Toward Fear: New Poems and a Poet's Handbook* (2004); *YellowBlack: The First Twenty-One Years of a Poet's Life, A Memoir* (2006); *Liberation Narratives: New and Collected Poems* 1966-2009 (2009); *Honoring Genius: Gwendolyn Brooks: The Narrative of Craft, Art, Kindness and Justice* (2011) and *By Any Means Necessary, Malcolm X: Real, Not Reinvented* (co-editor, 2012). Three book-length critical studies on Madhubuti's literary works are *New Directions from Don L. Lee* by Marlene Mosher (1975), *Malcolm X and the Poetics of Haki Madhubuti* by Regina Jennings (2006) and *Art of Work: The Art and Life of Haki R. Madhubuti* by Lita Hooper (2007). His poetry and essays were published in more than 100 anthologies and journals from 1997 to 2019. Madhubuti's book, *Taking Bullets: Terrorism and Black Life in Twenty-First Century America* was published in 2016 and he is the co-editor of *Not Our President: New Directions from the Pushed Out, the Others, and the Clear Majority in Trumps' Stolen America* (2017) and *Black Panther: Paradigm Shift or Not?* (2019).

Professor Madhubuti is a proponent of independent Black institutions. He founded Third World Press (1967) and Third World Press Foundation (2002). He is a founder of the Institute of Positive Education (1969, New Concept School (1972), co-founder of Betty Shabazz International Charter School (1998) and Barbara A. Sizemore Academy (2005), all of which are in Chicago and still operating. Madhubuti was founder and editor of Black Books Bulletin (1970-1994), a key journal documenting the literature, scholarship and conversations of African American voices for over two decades. He was also a founding member of the Organization of Black American Culture (OBAC) Writer's Workshop (1968). In 1977, he was the co-chair of North America's Mid-west Zone of FESTAC 77 (second world Black and African festival of art and culture). In this capacity, he helped to realize the dreams of many African American artists and scholars in facilitating their first trip to Africa (Lagos, Nigeria).

Professor Madhubuti is an award-winning poet and recipient of the National Endowment for the Arts and National Endowment for the Humanities fellowships, the American Book Award, Illinois Arts Council Award, Studs Terkel Humanities Service Award and others. In 1985, he was the only American poet chosen to represent the United States at the International Valmiki World Poetry Festival in New Delhi, India. In 2006, Madhubuti was awarded the "Literary Legacy Award" from the National Black Writers Conference at Medgar Evers College for creating and supporting Black literature and for building Black literary institutions. Madhubuti was named as a "2007 Chicagoan of the Year 'by *Chicago Magazine*. In May of 2008, Professor Madhubuti was honored with a "Lifetime Achievement Award" from Art Sanctuary of Philadelphia.

In 2009, he was named one of the "Ebony Power 150: Most Influential Blacks in America" for education. In 2010, he was presented with the President's Pacesetters Award from the American Association of Blacks in Higher Education and was awarded the Ninth Annual Hurston/Wright Legacy Award in poetry for his book, *Liberation Narratives*. At the 2013 Bridge Crossing Jubilee, Professor Haki R. Madhubuti was inducted into the "Hall of Resistance" at the Ancient Africa, Enslavement and Civil War Museum in Selma, Alabama. In 2014 he was inducted into the Arkansas Black Hall of Fame (along with President Bill Clinton) and also honored as the Arkansas Black "Hall of Fame 2014 Distinguished Laureate" presenter. In 2014, Dr. Madhubuti received the "Barnes & Noble Writers for Writers Award" presented by *Poets & Writers* magazine; and in April of that year, Dr. Madhubuti and wife, Dr. Carol D. Lee, were presented with the Du Sable Museum's Dogon Award at the "Night of 100 Stars" celebration. In June 2015, Madhubuti was the first poet to receive a "Lifetime Achievement Award" at the Juneteenth Book Festival Symposium at the Library of Congress; in September 2015, Madhubuti was honored by the Congressional Black Caucus Foundation with a "Lifetime Achievement Award for Leadership" in the Fine Arts; and in November of that same year, he received the Fuller Award from the Chicago Literary Hall of Fame. His most recent recognition includes the 2017 Go On Girl Book Club "Literary Legend Award" and the 2017 Sutton E. Griggs Tulisoma "Lifetime Achievement Award" in Literature in Dallas, Texas; 2017 he received the North Star Award from the Hurston/Wright Foundation, the foundation's highest honor for career accomplishment and inspiration to the writing community (along with Dr. Carla Hayden, the first woman and first African American to lead the Library of Congress and the late Congressman John Lewis). In June 2019, he received the Illinois Human Rights Commission (IHRC) "Activism in the Arts Award" during the celebration of Juneteenth; In 2020, the Nicolás Cristóbal Guillén Batista Lifetime Achievement Award from the Caribbean Philosophical Association.

Professor Madhubuti earned his MFA from the University of Iowa and received his third Doctor of Humane Letters from Spelman College in May of 2006. His distinguished teaching career includes faculty positions at Columbia College of Chicago (1967-68), Cornell University (1968-69), University of Illinois at Chicago (1969-70), Howard University (1970-78), Morgan State University (1973-74), University of Iowa (1982-1985). He is the former University Distinguished Professor and Professor of English at Chicago State University where he founded the Gwendolyn Brooks Center for Creative Writing and Black Literature. At Chicago State, Madhubuti also created the annual Gwendolyn Brooks Writers Conference (1989-2010) and was the founding director of the Master of Fine Arts in Creative Writing Program. Professor Madhubuti served as the last Ida B. Wells-Barnett Distinguished University Professor at DePaul University for 2010-11. His latest book of poetry is *Taught By Women: Poems As Resistance Language, New And Selected* (September 2020). He is currently completing the second volume of his autobiography, *New Music Screaming in the Sun*.

Photo courtesy of Raynard Graves

HAKI R. MADHUBUTI

PGIL2020USA